FIRST 50
CHRISTMAS CAROLS
YOU SHOULD PLAY ON GUITAR

ISBN 978-1-4950-9606-8

HAL•LEONARD®
7777 W. BLUEMOUND RD. P.O. BOX 13819 MILWAUKEE, WI 53213

In Australia Contact:
Hal Leonard Australia Pty. Ltd.
4 Lentara Court
Cheltenham, Victoria, 3192 Australia
Email: ausadmin@halleonard.com.au

Visit Hal Leonard Online at
www.halleonard.com

CONTENTS

Angels from the Realms of Glory

Words by James Montgomery
Music by Henry T. Smart

Key of C

Verse
Moderately

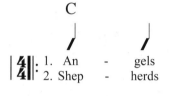 

C
1. An - gels from the | realms of glo - ry,
2. Shep - herds in the | field a - bid - ing,

F **C** **G7** **C**
| wing your flight o'er | all the earth.
| watch - ing o'er your | flocks by night,

E
Ye who sang cre - | a - tion's sto - ry,
God with man is | now re - sid - ing,

Am **G** **D7** **G**
| now pro - claim Mes - | si - ah's birth.
| yon - der shines the | in - fant light.

Chorus

G7 **C** **F**
| Come and wor - ship! | Come and wor - ship!

Dm **C G7 C** **C G7 C**
| Wor - ship Christ the | new - born King! :| new - born King!

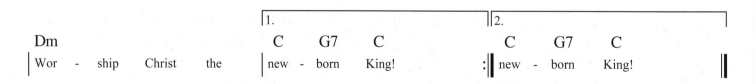

Angels We Have Heard on High

Traditional French Carol
Translated by James Chadwick

Melody:

An - gels we have heard on high,

G   D   D7   E   Am   C

Key of G

Verse

Moderately

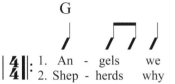

G				D		G	
1. An - gels	we	have	heard	on	high,	sweet - ly	sing - ing
2. Shep - herds	why	this	ju -	bi -	lee,	why	your joy - ous

D7	G				D	G	
o'er	the plains.	And	the moun - tains	in	re - ply,	ech - o - ing	their
strains	pro - long?	What	the glad - some	ti -	dings be	which in -	spire your

Chorus

D7	G		G	E	Am	D	G	C
joy - ous strains.			Glo		-			
heav'n - ly song?								

D7		G		D		G	E
-	ri - a	in ex - cel - sis	De -		o.	Glo	-

Am	D	G	C	D7		G	E
		-			ri - a	in ex - cel - sis	

1.		D7	G	2.		D7	G
De	-		o.	De	-		o.

As with Gladness Men of Old

Words by William Chatterton Dix
Music by Conrad Kocher

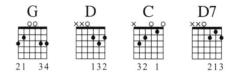

Key of G

Verse

Moderately fast

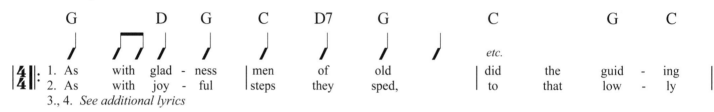

1. As	with	glad -	ness	men	of	old	did	the	guid - ing
2. As	with	joy -	ful	steps	they	sped,	to	that	low - ly

star	be -	hold;	as	with	joy	they	hailed its	light,
man -	ger	bed,	there	to	bend	the	knee be -	fore

lead -	ing	on - ward,	beam -	ing	bright;	so,	most gra - cious
Him	who	Heav'n and	Earth	a -	dore,	so	may we with

1., 2., 3. | **4.**

Lord,	may	we	ev -	er - more	be	led	to Thee.	glo - ry hide.
will -	ing	feet	ev -	er	seek thy	mer -	cy seat.	

Additional Lyrics

3. As they offered gifts most rare
   At that manger rude and bare,
   So may we with holy joy,
   Pure and free from sin's alloy,
   All our costliest treasures bring,
   Christ, to Thee, our heavenly King.

4. Holy Jesus, every day
   Keep us in the narrow way;
   And, when earthly things are past,
   Bring our ransomed souls at last
   Where they need no star to guide,
   Where no clouds Thy glory hide.

Auld Lang Syne

Words by Robert Burns
Traditional Scottish Melody

Key of G

Verse
Moderately

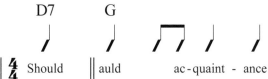 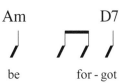

D7	G		Am	D7	Em	G7
Should	auld	ac-quaint - ance	be	for-got and	nev -	er brought to

etc.

C		G		Am	B7	
mind?	Should	auld	ac-quaint - ance	be	for - got and	

Chorus

Em	Am	D7	G	D7	G	
days	of Auld	Lang	Syne?	For	Auld	Lang

Am	D7	G	G7	C	
Syne,	my dear, for	Auld	Lang	Syne.	We'll

G	Am	B7	Em	Am D7 G	
take a cup of	kind - ness yet for	Auld	Lang	Syne.	

Away in a Manger

Words by John T. McFarland (v.3)
Music by James R. Murray

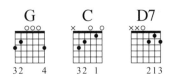

Key of G

Verse

Moderately

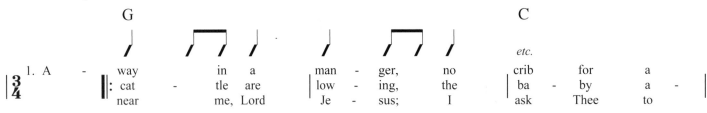

1. A - way in a man - ger, no crib for a
: cat - tle are low - ing, the ba - by a -
near me, Lord Je - sus; I ask Thee to

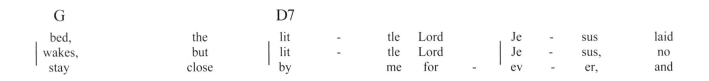

bed, the lit - tle Lord Je - sus laid
wakes, but lit - tle Lord Je - sus, no
stay close by me for - ev - er, and

down His sweet head. The stars in the
cry - ing He makes. I love thee, Lord
love me, I pray. Bless all the dear

sky looked down where he lay. The lit - tle Lord
Je - sus, look down from the sky and stay by my
chil - dren in Thy ten - der care, and take us to

1., 2.   **3.**

Je - sus, a - sleep on the hay. 2. The there.
cra - dle 'til morn - ing is nigh. 3. Be
heav - en, to live with Thee

Bring a Torch, Jeanette, Isabella

17th Century French Provencal Carol

Melody:

Bring a torch, ____ Jean - ette,

G   Am   D   D7   C   Em

Key of G

Verse

Moderately fast

G

1. Bring a torch, Jean - ette, Is - a - | Am bel - | D la;
2. Hast - en now, good folk of the | vil - | lage,

G
bring a torch, come the | D7 swift - ly and | G run.
hast - en now, the Christ Child to see.

Christ is born, tell the folk of the | vil - | D lage,
You will find him a - sleep in a man - ger,

C
Je - sus is | G sleep - ing | D7 in His | G cra - dle.
qui - et - ly come and whis - per soft - ly.

Em | D | G | D | G
Ah, | ah, | beau - ti - ful | is the | Moth - er.
Hush, | hush, | peace - ful - ly | now He | slum - bers.

Em | D | G | D
Ah, | ah, | beau - ti - ful | is her
Hush, | hush, | peace - ful - ly | now He

1.
G
| Son. |

2.
G
:| sleeps. |

Canon in D

By Johann Pachelbel

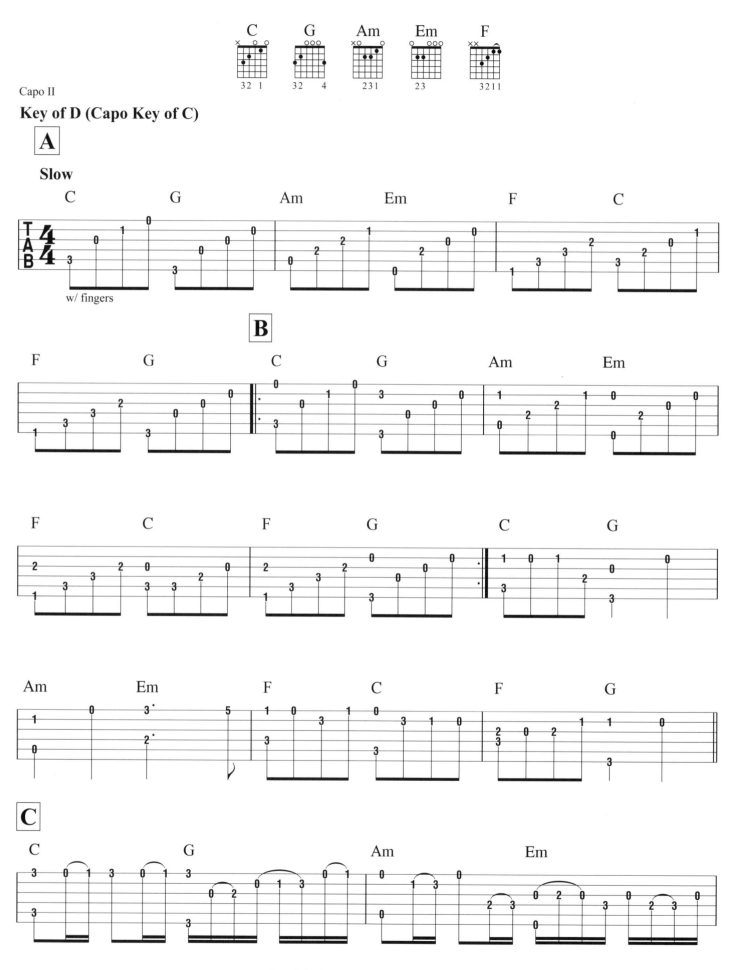

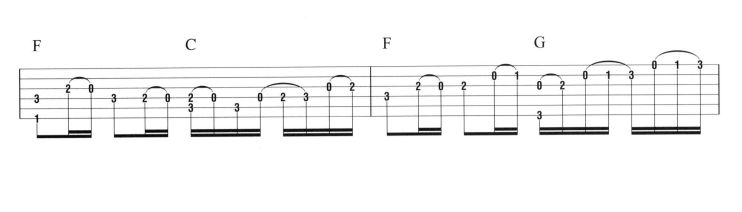

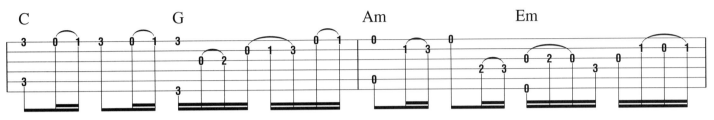

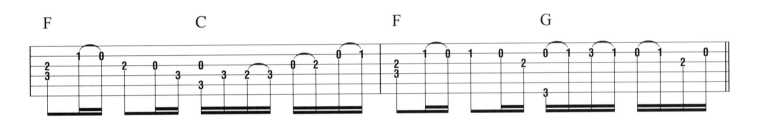

D

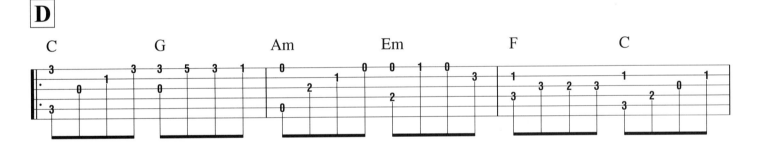

E

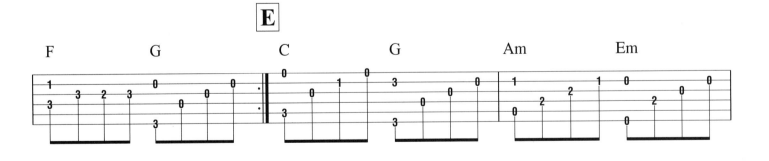

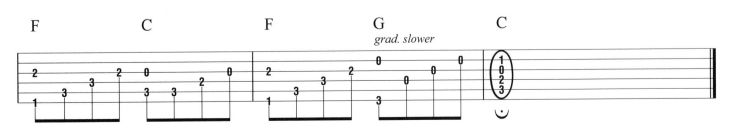

A Child Is Born in Bethlehem

14th-Century Latin Text adapted by Nicolai F.S. Grundtvig
Traditional Danish Melody

Melody:

A Child is born in Beth - le - hem,

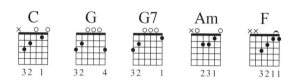

C   G   G7   Am   F

32 1   32 4   32 1   231   3211

Key of C

Moderately slow   **Verse**

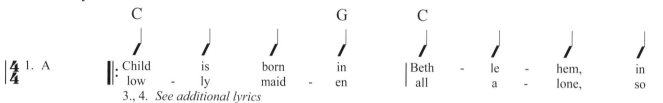

4/4   1. A   │: Child   is   born   in   │ Beth - le - hem,   in

low - ly   maid - en   all   a - lone, so

3., 4. See additional lyrics

G   G7   C

etc.

│ Beth - le - hem;   and   │ joy   is   in   Je -

all   a - lone,   gave   birth   to   God's   own

Am   G7   C   F   C   G

│ ru - sa - lem.   ⎱   Al - │ le - lu - ia,   al - │ le - lu -

Ho - ly   Son.   ⎰

1., 2., 3.

C   C   G   C

│ ia!   2. A   :│ le - lu - │ ia!

4.

Additional Lyrics

3. She chose a manger for His bed,
For Jesus' bed.
God's angels sang for joy o'erhead.
Alleluia, alleluia!

4. Give thanks and praise eternally,
Eternally,
To God, the Holy Trinity.
Alleluia, alleluia!

Christ Was Born on Christmas Day

Traditional

Melody:

Christ was born on Christ - mas Day,

 G   C   Am   D7   D

Key of G

Verse
Moderately slow, in 2

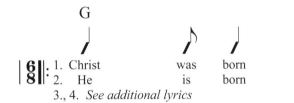 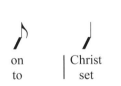 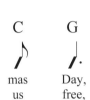

G   C   G

| 1. Christ | was | born | on | Christ | - | mas | Day, |
| 2. He | is | born | to | set | | us | free, |

3., 4. *See additional lyrics*

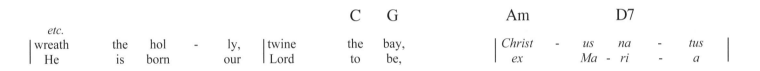

                                         C   G   Am   D7

etc.

| wreath | the | hol - | ly, | twine | the | bay, | *Christ* | - | *us* | *na* | - | *tus* |
| He | is | born | our | Lord | to | be, | *ex* | | *Ma* | - | *ri* | - | *a* |

G   D   G   C   G   D7

| *ho* | - | *di* | - | *e;* | the | Babe, | the | Son, | the | Ho | - | ly | One | of |
| *Vir* | - | *gi* | - | *ne;* | the | God, | the | Lord, | by | all | | a - | dored | for - |

| 1., 2., 3.   **| 4.**

G   G

| Mar | - | y. | | Mar | - | y. |
| ev | - | er. | | | | |

Additional Lyrics

3. Let the bright red berries glow,
   Ev'rywhere in goodly show;
   Christus natus hodie;
   The Babe, the Son, the Holy One of Mary.

4. Christian men rejoice and sing,
   'Tis the birthday of a King,
   Ex Maria Virgine;
   The God, the Lord, by all adored forever.

Coventry Carol

Words by Robert Croo
Traditional English Melody

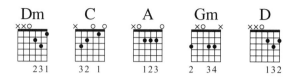

Key of Dm

Verse

Moderately

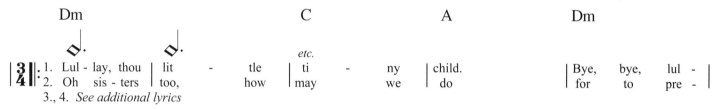

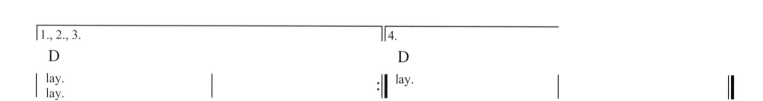

Gm	Dm		C	
ly,	lul -	lay.	Lul -	lay,	thou	lit -	tle
serve	this	day	this	poor	young -	ling	for

Gm	A	Dm	Gm
ti -	ny	child.	Bye,	bye,	lul -	ly,	lul -
whom	we	sing?	Bye,	bye,	lul -	ly,	lul -

1., 2., 3.

D

| lay. | |
| lay. | |

4.

D

| lay. | |

Additional Lyrics

3. Herod the King, in his raging,
   Charged he hath this day
   His men of might in his own sight
   All young children to slay.

4. That woe is me, poor child for thee,
   And ever morn and day,
   For thy parting neither say nor sing
   Bye, bye, lully, lullay.

Deck the Hall

Traditional Welsh Carol

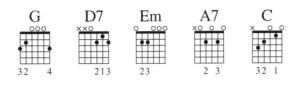

Key of G

Verse
Moderately fast

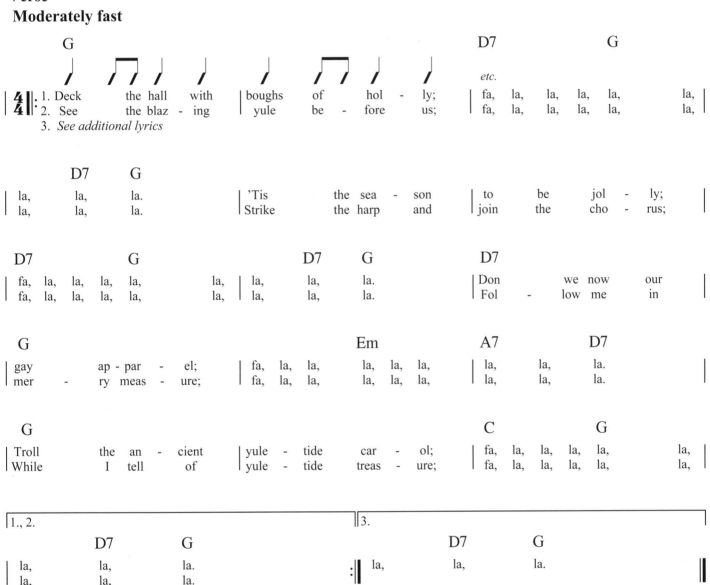

Additional Lyrics

3. Fast away the old year passes;
Fa, la, la, la, la, la, la, la, la.
Hail the new ye lads and lasses;
Fa, la, la, la, la, la, la, la, la.
Sing we joyous, all together;
Fa, la, la, la, la, la, la, la, la.
Heedless of the wind and weather;
Fa, la, la, la, la, la, la, la, la.

Ding Dong! Merrily on High!

French Carol

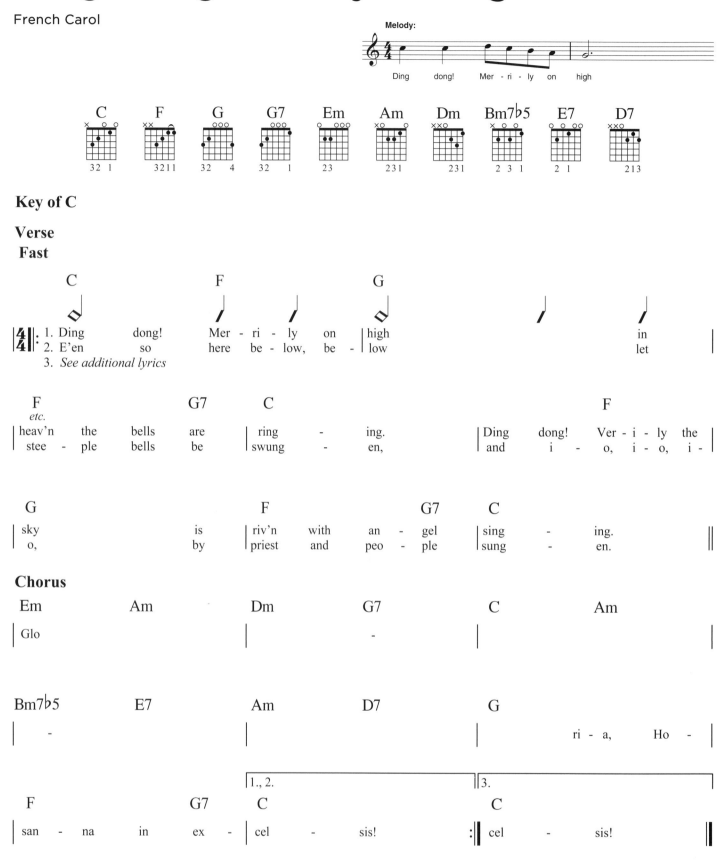

Key of C

Verse

Fast

1. Ding dong! Mer - ri - ly on high in
2. E'en so here be - low, be - low let
3. *See additional lyrics*

etc.

heav'n the bells are ring - ing. Ding dong! Ver - i - ly the
stee - ple bells be swung - en, and i - o, i - o, i -

sky is riv'n with an - gel sing - ing.
o, by priest and peo - ple sung - en.

Chorus

Glo

ri - a, Ho -

1., 2.

san - na in ex - cel - sis!

3.

cel - sis!

Additional Lyrics

3. Pray you dutifully prime
Your matin chime, ye ringers;
May you beautifully rime
Your evetime song, ye singers.

The First Noël

17th Century English Carol
Music from W. Sandys' Christmas Carols

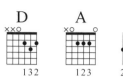 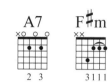

Key of D

Verse
Moderately slow

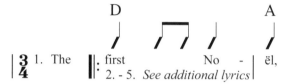 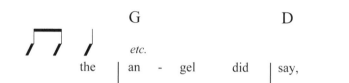

D		A		G		D
1. The	first	No -	ël,	the an - gel did	say,	was to

2. - 5. *See additional lyrics*

G		D	A7	D	A7	D
cer - tain poor	shep - herds in	fields as they	lay.	In

	A		G	D	
fields	where they	lay	keep - ing their	sheep,	on a

G		D	A7	D	A7	D
cold win - ter's	night	that was	so	deep.	No -

Chorus

D	F#m		G	D	
ël,	No -	ël,	No -	ël,	No -	ël,

G		D	A7	D	A7	D	D
born is the	King	of Is - ra - el.	2. They	ël.	el.

1. - 4.   5.

Additional Lyrics

2. They looked up and saw a star
   Shining in the east, beyond them far.
   And to the earth it gave great light
   And so it continued both day and night.

3. And by the light of that same star,
   Three wise men came from country far;
   To seek for a King was their intent,
   And to follow the star wherever it went.

4. This star drew nigh to the northwest,
   O'er Bethlehem it took its rest;
   And there it did both stop and stay,
   Right over the place where Jesus lay.

5. Then entered in those wise men three,
   Fell reverently upon their knee,
   And offered there in His presence,
   Their gold and myrrh and frankincense.

The Friendly Beasts

Traditional English Carol

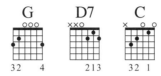

Key of G

Verse
Moderately

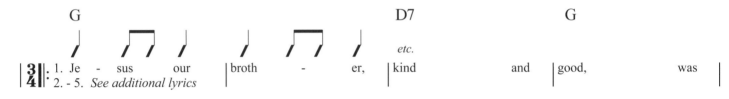

G				D7	G
1. Je - sus our	broth - er,	kind and	good,	was
2. - 5. *See additional lyrics*				

	C		D7	G
hum - bly	born	in a	sta - ble	rude, and the

	C		D7	G
friend - ly	beasts	a - round	Him	stood,

	D7	G *1. - 5.*	G *6.*
Je - sus our	broth - er,	kind and	good.	el.

Additional Lyrics

2. "I," said the donkey, shaggy and brown,
   "I carried his mother up hill and down.
   I carried his mother to Bethlehem town."
   "I," said the donkey, shaggy and brown.

3. "I," said the cow, all white and red,
   "I gave Him my manger for His bed.
   I gave Him my hay to pillow His head."
   "I," said the cow, all white and red.

4. "I," said the sheep with the curly horn,
   "I gave Him my wool for His blanket warm.
   He wore my coat on Christmas morn."
   "I," said the sheep with the curly horn.

5. "I," said the dove from the rafters high,
   "I cooed Him to sleep that He would not cry.
   We cooed Him to sleep, my mate and I."
   "I," said the dove from the rafters high.

6. Thus every beast by some good spell,
   In the stable dark was glad to tell
   Of the gift he gave Emmanuel,
   The gift he gave Emmanuel.

Fum, Fum, Fum

Traditional Catalonian Carol

Key of Am

Verse

Moderately, in 2

Am			Dm	E7	Am	E7	
1. On	this joy - ful		Christ - mas day, sing		fum,	fum,	
2. Thanks	to God for		hol - i - days, sing		fum,	fum,	

Am				Dm	E7	
fum.		*etc.* On	this joy - ful	Christ - mas day, sing		
fum.		Thanks	to God for	hol - i - days, sing		

Am	E7	Am		C	G7	
fum,	fum,	fum.	For a	bless - ed Babe was		
fum,	fum,	fum.	Now we	all our voic - es		

C			G7	C		
born up - on this	day at	break of	morn.	In a		
raise and sing a	song of	grate - ful	praise.	Cel - e -		

F	Dm	E7		Am	Dm	
man - ger poor and	low - ly lay the	Son of God most				**2/4**
brate in song and	sto - ry all the	won - ders of His				

E7	Am	E7	1. Am	2. Am	
2/4 ho - ly.	Fum, fum,	fum.		fum.	
glo - ry.	Fum, fum,				

Gather Around the Christmas Tree

By John H. Hopkins

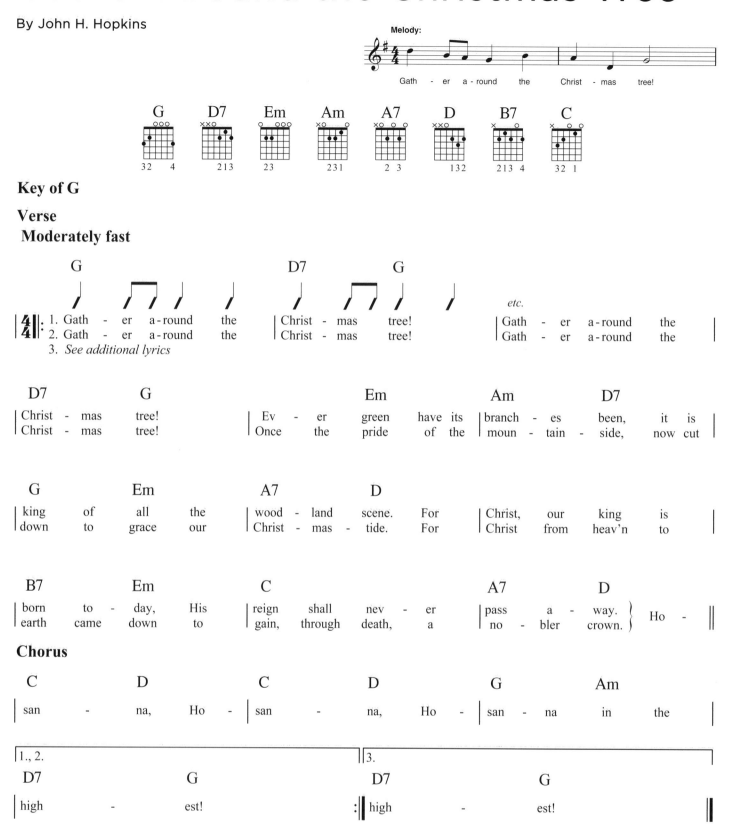

Key of G

Verse

Moderately fast

Additional Lyrics

3. Gather around the Christmas tree!
Gather around the Christmas tree!
Ev'ry bough has a burden now,
They are gifts of love for us, we trow.
For Christ is born, his love to show
And give good gifts to men below.

Go, Tell It on the Mountain

African-American Spiritual
Verses by John W. Work, Jr.

Melody:

Go, tell it on the moun - tain,

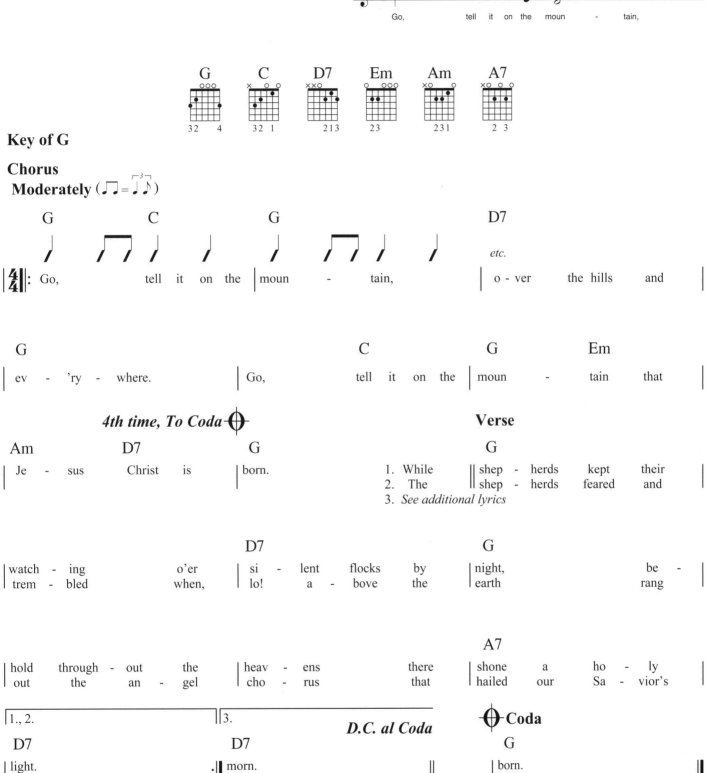

Key of G

Chorus
Moderately

G		C	G		D7
Go,		tell it on the	moun - tain,		o - ver the hills and

etc.

G		C	G	Em
ev - 'ry - where.	Go,	tell it on the	moun - tain that	

4th time, To Coda ⊕

Verse

Am	D7	G		G
Je - sus	Christ is	born.		1. While shep - herds kept their
				2. The shep - herds feared and

3. *See additional lyrics*

	D7		G
watch - ing o'er	si - lent flocks by	night,	be -
trem - bled when,	lo! a - bove the	earth	rang

		A7
hold through - out the	heav - ens there	shone a ho - ly
out the an - gel	cho - rus that	hailed our Sa - vior's

1., 2.	3.	*D.C. al Coda*	⊕ **Coda**
D7	D7		G
light.	morn.		born.
birth.			

Additional Lyrics

3. Down in a lowly manger
   Our humble Christ was born
   And God sent us salvation
   That blessed Christmas morn.

God Rest Ye Merry, Gentlemen

Traditional English Carol

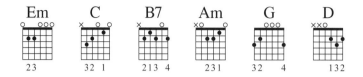

Key of Em

Verse

Moderately

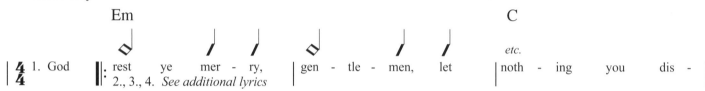

Em						C
1. God	rest ye mer - ry,	gen - tle - men, let	noth - ing you dis -			
	2., 3., 4. *See additional lyrics*					

B7		Em				
may.	Re -	mem - ber Christ our	Sav - ior was			

C		B7		Am		
born on Christ - mas	day	to	save us all from			

G		Em		D		
Sa - tan's pow'r when	we were gone a -	stray. O				

Chorus

G		B7		Em		D
tid - ings of	com - fort and	joy, com-fort and	joy. O			

				1., 2., 3.		4.
G		B7		Em		Em
tid - ings of	com - fort and	joy. 2. In	joy.			

Additional Lyrics

2. In Bethlehem, in Jewry, this blessed Babe was born
   And laid within a manger upon this blessed morn
   That which His mother Mary did nothing take in scorn.

3. From God, our heav'nly Father, a blessed angel came
   And unto certain shepherds brought tidings of the same.
   How that in Bethlehem was born the Son of God by name.

4. Now shepherds, at those tidings, rejoiced much in mind
   And left their flocks a feeding in tempest, storm and wind
   And went to Bethlehem straightway the Son of God to find.

Good Christian Men, Rejoice

14th Century Latin Text
Translated by John Mason Neale
14th Century German Melody

Key of G

G   Em   C   Am7   D7

Verse

Moderately slow, in 2

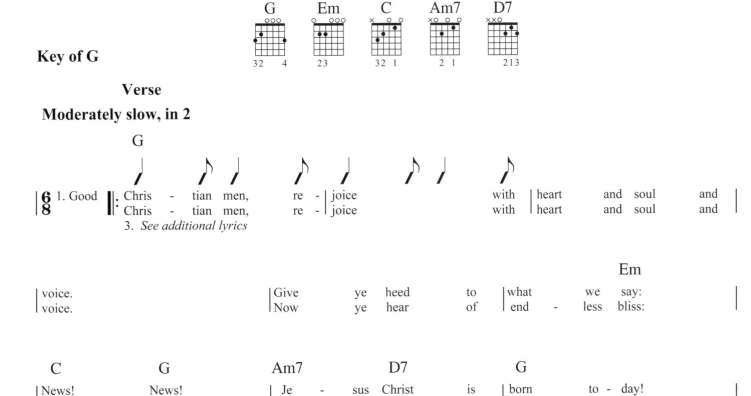

G

1. Good	Chris - tian men,	re - joice	with	heart	and	soul	and
	Chris - tian men,	re - joice	with	heart	and	soul	and
	3. *See additional lyrics*						

| voice. | | | | Give | ye | heed | to | what | we | say: | **Em** |
| voice. | | | | Now | ye | hear | of | end - | less | bliss: | |

C   **G**   **Am7**   **D7**   **G**

| News! | News! | Je - | sus Christ | is | born | to - day! |
| Joy! | Joy! | Je - | sus Christ | was | born | for this. |

                                                 Em   **Am7**   **D7**

| Ox | and | ass | be - | fore | Him | bow, | and | He | is | in | the |
| He | hath | op'd | the | heav'n - | ly | door, | and | man | is | bless - | ed |

G   **C**   **D7**   **G**   **D7**

| man - | ger | now. | Christ | is | born | to - | day! |
| ev - | er - more. | | Christ | was | born | for | this! |

1., 2.   **3.**

G   **D7**   **G**   **G**

| Christ | is | born | to - | day! | 2. Good | save! |
| Christ | was | born | for | this! | 3. Good | |

Additional Lyrics

3. Good Christian men, rejoice
   With heart and soul and voice.
   Now ye need not fear the grave: Peace! Peace!
   Jesus Christ was born to save!
   Calls you one and calls you all,
   To gain His everlasting hall.
   Christ was born to save!
   Christ was born to save!

Good King Wenceslas

Words by John M. Neale
Music from Piae Cantiones

Melody:

Good King Wen - ces - las looked out

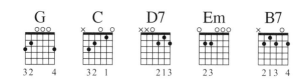

G   C   D7   Em   B7

Key of G

Verse
Moderately, in 2

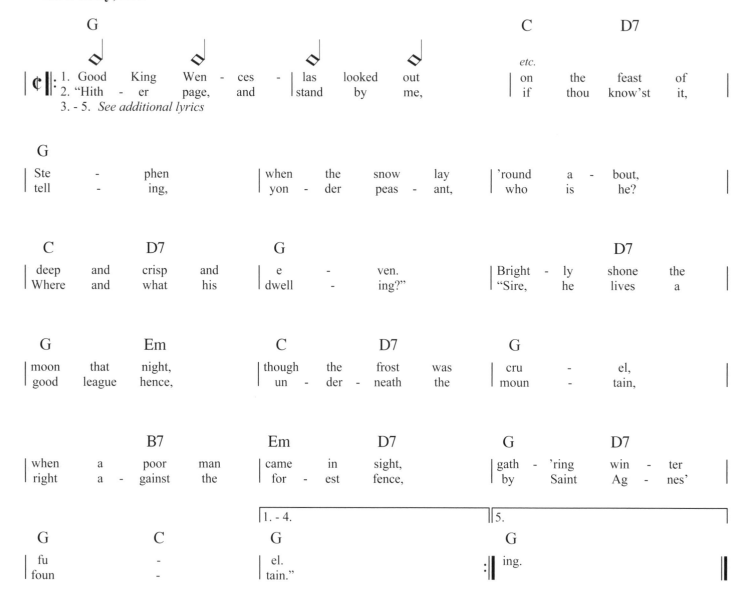

G				C	D7
1. Good King Wen - ces - las	looked out	on the feast of
2. "Hith - er page, and	stand by me,	if thou know'st it,
3. - 5. *See additional lyrics*		

G					
Ste - phen	when the snow lay	'round a - bout,
tell - ing,	yon - der peas - ant,	who is he?

C	D7	G			D7
deep and crisp and	e - ven.	Bright - ly shone the
Where and what his	dwell - ing?"	"Sire, he lives a

G	Em	C	D7	G	
moon that night,	though the frost was	cru - el,
good league hence,	un - der - neath the	moun - tain,

	B7	Em	D7	G	D7
when a poor man	came in sight,	gath - 'ring win - ter
right a - gainst the	for - est fence,	by Saint Ag - nes'

1. - 4.

G	C	G
fu -	el.
foun -	tain."

5.

G
ing.

Additional Lyrics

3. "Bring me flesh, and bring me wine;
   Bring me pine-logs hither.
   Thou and I will see him dine
   When we bear them thither."
   Page and monarch, forth they went,
   Forth they went together,
   Through the rude wind's wild lament
   And the bitter weather.

4. "Sire, the night is darker now,
   And the wind blows stronger.
   Fails my heart, I know not how;
   I can go not longer."
   "Mark my footsteps, my good page;
   Tread thou in them boldly.
   Thou shalt find the winter's rage
   Freeze thy blood less coldly."

5. In his master's steps he trod,
   Where the snow lay dinted;
   Heat was in the very sod
   Which the saint has printed.
   Therefore, Christian men, be sure,
   Wealth or rank possessing,
   Ye who now will bless the poor
   Shall yourselves find blessing.

Hark! The Herald Angels Sing

Words by Charles Wesley
Altered by George Whitefield
Music by Felix Mendelssohn-Bartholdy

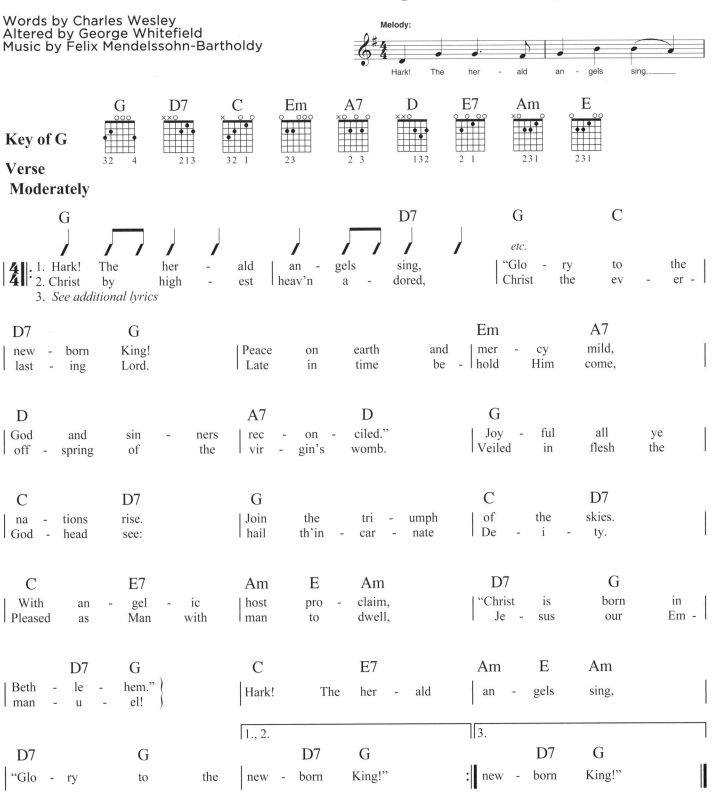

Key of G

Verse

Moderately

Additional Lyrics

Hail, the heav'n-born Prince of Peace!
Hail, the Son of Righteousness!
Light and life to all He brings,
Ris'n with healing in His wings.
Mild he lays His glory by,
Born that man no more may die.
Born to raise the sons of earth,
Born to give them second birth.
Hark! The herald angels sing,
"Glory to the newborn King!"

Hear Them Bells

Words and Music by D.S. McCosh

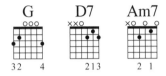

Key of G

Verse

Moderately, in 2

| **G** | | | | **D7** | **G** | |

Hear them bells, _____ mer - ry Christ - mas bells!

| | | **Am7** | | | **D7** | |

They are ring - ing out the e - vil of the

| **G** | | | | | |

sword. Hear them bells,

| | **D7** | **G** | | | |

mer - ry Christ - mas bells! They are

| **Am7** | **D7** | **G** | | |

ring - ing in the glo - ry of the Lord!

Here We Come A-Wassailing

Traditional

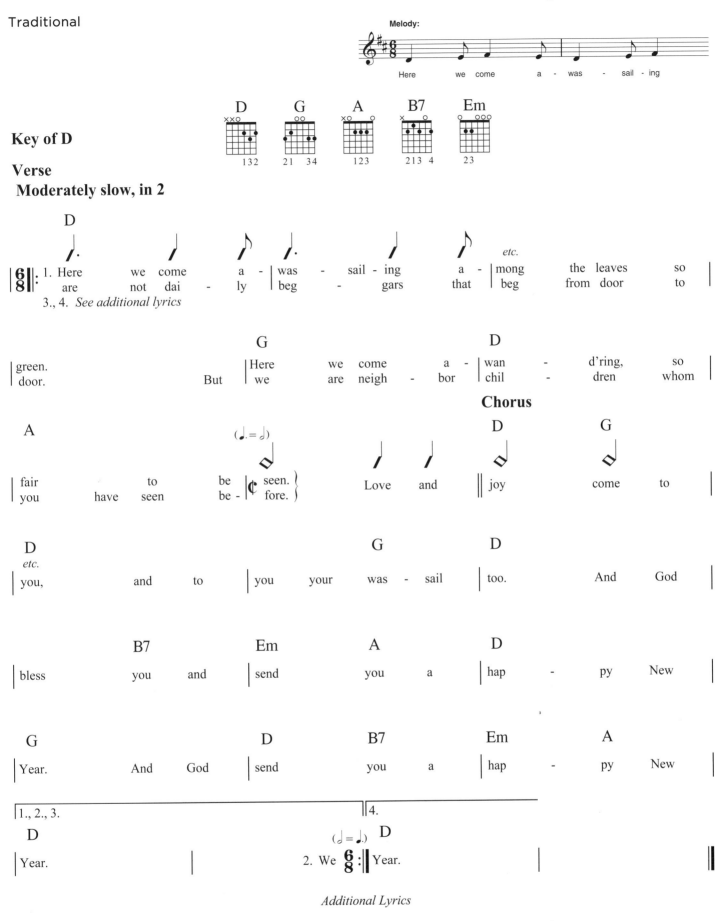

Key of D

Verse
Moderately slow, in 2

1. Here we come a- was - sail - ing a - mong the leaves so
   are not dai - ly beg - gars that beg from door to

3., 4. *See additional lyrics*

green. But Here we come a - wan - d'ring, so
door. we are neigh - bor chil - dren so whom

Chorus

fair to be seen. Love and joy come to
you have seen be - fore.

etc.
you, and to you your was - sail too. And God

bless you and send you a hap - py New

Year. And God send you a hap - py New

1., 2., 3.
D
Year.

4.
2. We Year.

Additional Lyrics

3. We have got a little purse
   Of stretching leather skin.
   We want a little money
   To line it well within.

4. God bless the master of this house,
   Likewise the mistress too,
   And all the little children
   That round the table go.

The Holly and the Ivy

18th Century English Carol

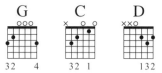

Key of G

Verse

Moderately

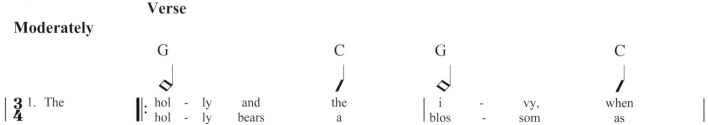

|| The hol - ly and the i - vy, when
  hol - ly bears a blos - som as

3. See additional lyrics

etc.

they are both full grown, of all the trees that are
white as lil - y flow'r, and Mar - y bore sweet

in the wood, the hol - ly bears the crown.} The
Je - sus Christ to be our sweet Sav - ior.}

Chorus

ris - ing of the sun and the run - ning of the

deer. The play - ing of the mer - ry or - gan, sweet

1., 2. | **3.**

sing - ing of the choir. 2. The :|| choir.

Additional Lyrics

3. The holly bears a berry
   As red as any blood,
   And Mary bore sweet Jesus Christ
   To do poor sinners good.

I Heard the Bells on Christmas Day

Words by Henry Wadsworth Longfellow
Music by John Baptiste Calkin

Key of G

Moderately

Verse

 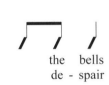 

G				C		D7	
heard	the bells	on		Christ-	mas	Day,	their
in	de-spair	I		bowed	my	head;	"There

Em		F#7	Bm		Am		D7
old	fa-mil-iar	car-ols	play;	and	wild	and sweet	the
is	no peace on	earth," I	said,	"for	hate	is strong	and

Bm7♭5	E7	Am			A7	D7	
words	re-peat of	peace	on	earth, good	will	to men.	I
mocks	the song of	peace	on	earth, good	will	to men."	Then

G		C	D7	Em		
thought,	as now this	day	had come, the	bel-	fries of	all
pealed	the bells this	more	loud and deep;	"God	is	not dead, nor

F#7	Bm	Am	D7	Bm7♭5	E7	
Chris-ten-dom	had	rung	so long the un-	bro-	ken song of	
doth He	sleep. The	wrong	shall fail, the	right	pre-vail with	

1.

Am		D7	G	2. D7	G	
peace	on earth, good	will	to men 2. And	will	to men."	
peace	on earth, good					

I Saw Three Ships

Traditional English Carol

Melody:

I saw three ships come sail-ing in

 G   D

21 34   132

Key of G

Verse

Moderately slow, in 2

 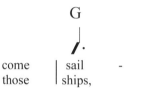

		G		D		G		D	
6/8	1. I	saw	three ships	come	sail	- ing	in	on
		what	was	in	those	ships,	all	three,	on

G			D			G			D	
etc.										
Christ	- mas Day,	on	Christ	- mas	day;	I	saw	three ships	come
Christ	- mas Day,	on	Christ	- mas	day;	and	what	was in	those

G		D		G					1.	D		G		
sail	- ing	in	on	Christ	- mas Day	in the	morn	- ing.	2. And					
ships,	all three,	on	Christ	- mas Day	in the									

2.	D		G		**Verse**	G		D		G		D	
morn	- ing?	3. The		Vir	- gin Mar - y	and	Christ	were there	on				

G			D			G			D	
Christ	- mas Day,	on	Christ	- mas Day;	the	Vir	- gin Mar - y	and	

G		D		G			D		G	
Christ	were there	on	Christ	- mas Day	in the	morn	- ing.	

In the Bleak Midwinter

Poem by Christina Rossetti
Music by Gustav Holst

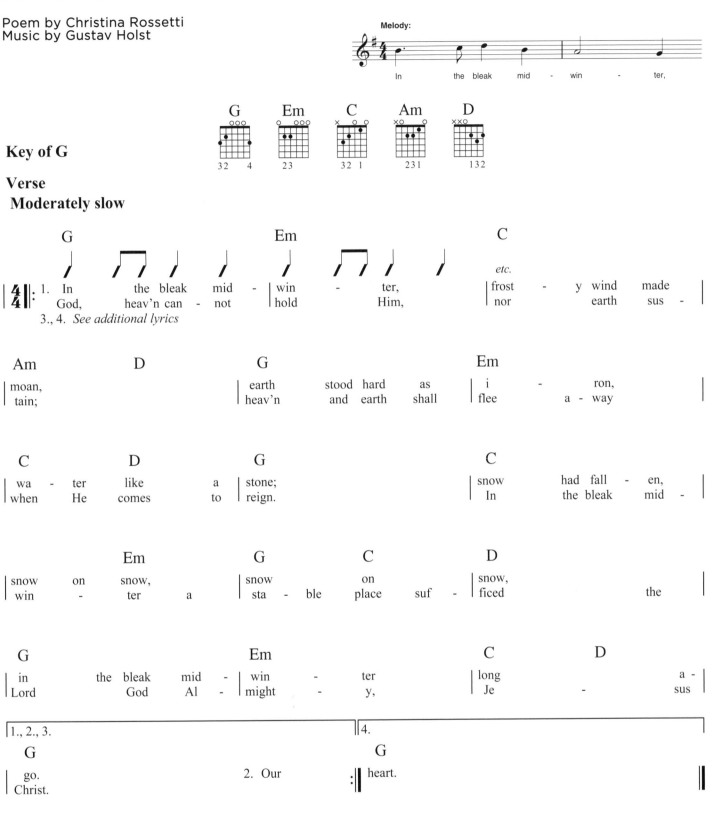

Key of G

Verse
Moderately slow

Additional Lyrics

3. Angels and archangels may have gathered there,
Cherubim and seraphim thronged the air;
But his mother only, in her maiden bliss,
Worshipped the beloved with a kiss.

4. What can I give him, poor as I am?
If I were a shepherd, I would bring a lamb;
If I were a Wise Man, I would do my part;
Yet what can I give him: give my heart.

It Came Upon the Midnight Clear

Words by Edmund Hamilton Sears
Music by Richard Storrs Willis

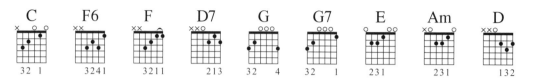

Key of C

Verse
Moderately fast

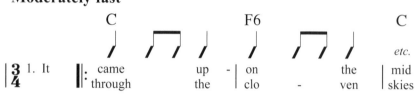

C			F6			C		
1. It	came	up	on	the	mid	-	night	clear,	that
through	the	clo	-	ven	skies	they	come,	with

F			D7			G		G7		C	
glo	-	ri	-	ous	song	of	old,		from	an	-	gels
peace	-	ful	wings	un	-	furled,		and	still	their

F6			C				F		G	
bend	-	ing	near	the	earth,	to	touch	their	harps	of
heav'n	-	ly	mu	-	sic	floats,	o'er	all	the	wea	-	ry

C			E				Am		
gold.		"Peace	on	the	earth,	good	will	to
world.	A	-	bove	its	sad	and	low	-	ly

G		D			G		G7	
men,	from	heav	-	en's	all	gra	-	cious	King."	The
plains	they	bend	on	hov	-	er	-	ing	wing,	and

C		F6			C				F	
world	in	sol	-	emn	still	-	ness	lay,	to	hear	the
ev	-	er	o'er	its	Ba	-	bel	sounds	the	bless	-	ed

G			C				C	
1.						2.		
an	-	gels	sing.		2. Still	sing.
an	-	gels				

Jingle Bells

Words and Music by J. Pierpont

Key of G

Verse
   Moderately, in 2

G   C   D7   A7

G								C
1. Dash - ing through the	snow		in a	one horse o - pen	sleigh,			
2., 3. *See additional lyrics*								

etc.

			D7					G	
o'er the fields we	go,			laugh - ing all the	way.				

Bells on bob - tail	ring,			mak - ing spir - its	bright.	What		C

			D7					G	
fun it is to	ride and sing a	sleigh - ing song to -	night!	Oh,					

Chorus

  G

jin - gle bells,	jin - gle bells,	jin - gle all the	way.	

C		G		A7		D7
Oh, what fun it	is to ride in a	one horse o - pen	sleigh!	

G				C
Jin - gle bells,	jin - gle bells,	jin - gle all the	way.	Oh, what fun it

                                  1., 2.   **3.**

G		D7		G			G
is to ride in a	one horse o - pen	sleigh!	2. A	sleigh!	

Additional Lyrics

2. A day or two ago, I thought I'd take a ride,
   And soon Miss Fannie Bright was sitting by my side.
   The horse was lean and lank,
   Misfortune seemed his lot.
   He got into a drifted bank and then we got upsot!

3. Now the ground is white, go it while you're young.
   Take the girls tonight and sing this sleighing song.
   Just get a bobtail bay, two-forty for his speed,
   Then hitch him to an open sleigh and
   Crack, you'll take the lead!

Jolly Old St. Nicholas

Traditional 19th Century American Carol

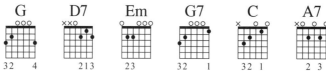

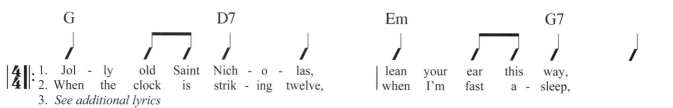

Key of G

Verse

Moderately slow

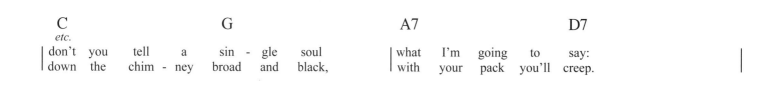

G		D7		Em		G7
1. Jol - ly old Saint Nich - o - las,				lean your ear this way,		
2. When the clock is strik - ing twelve,				when I'm fast a - sleep,		

3. *See additional lyrics*

C		G		A7		D7
etc. don't you tell a sin - gle soul				what I'm going to say:		
down the chim - ney broad and black,				with your pack you'll creep.		

G		D7		Em		G7
Christ - mas Eve is com - ing soon,				now, you dear old man,		
All the stock - ings you will find				hang - ing in a row,		

C	G	1., 2. A7	D7	G	3. A7	D7	G
whis - per what you'll bring to me;		tell me if you can.			what you think is right.		
mine will be the short - est one;		you'll be sure to know.					

Additional Lyrics

3. Johnny wants a pair of skates; Susy wants a sled.
   Nellie wants a picture book, yellow, blue and red.
   Now I think I'll leave to you what to give the rest.
   Choose for me, dear Santa Claus. You will know the best.

Joy to the World

Words by Isaac Watts
Music by George Frideric Handel
Adapted by Lowell Mason

Melody:
Joy to the world!

D   A7   G

Key of D

Verse
Moderately slow, in 2

D					A7	D	
1. Joy	to	the	world!	The	Lord is	come;	let
2. Joy	to	the	world!	The	Sav - ior	reigns;	let

3., 4. *See additional lyrics*

etc.

G		A7		D			G
earth	re -	ceive	her	King.	Let	ev -	'ry
men	their	songs	em -	ploy	while	fields	and

D		G	D			
heart	pre -	pare Him	room,	and	heav-en and na - ture
floods,	rocks,	hills and	plains	re -	peat the sound - ing

		A7			D	
sing,	and	heav-en and na - ture	sing,	and	heav - en	and
joy,	re -	peast the sound - ing	joy,	re -	peat,	re -

		A7	D	1., 2., 3.	4. D
heav - en and	na - ture	sing.		love.
peat the	sound - ing	joy.		

Additional Lyrics

3. No more let sin and sorrow grow,
   Nor thorns infest the ground;
   He comes to make
   His blessings flow
   Far as the curse is found,
   Far as the curse is found,
   Far as, far as the curse is found.

4. He rules the world with truth and grace
   And makes the nations prove
   The glories of
   His righteousness
   And wonders of His love,
   And wonders of His love,
   And wonders, wonders of His love.

March

from THE NUTCRACKER

By Pyotr Il'yich Tchaikovsky

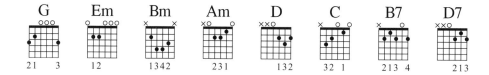

Key of G

Moderately

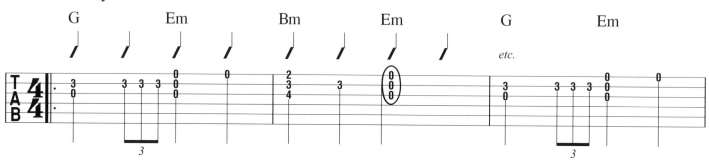

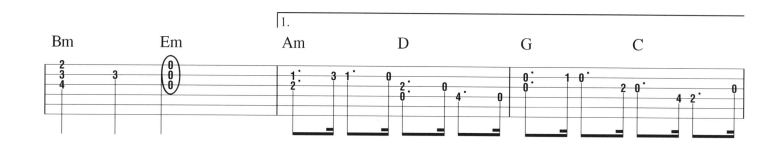

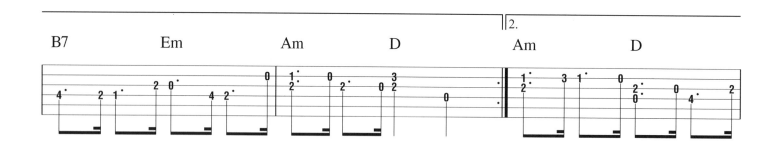

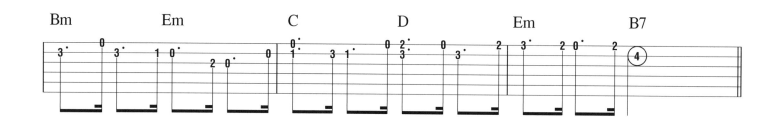

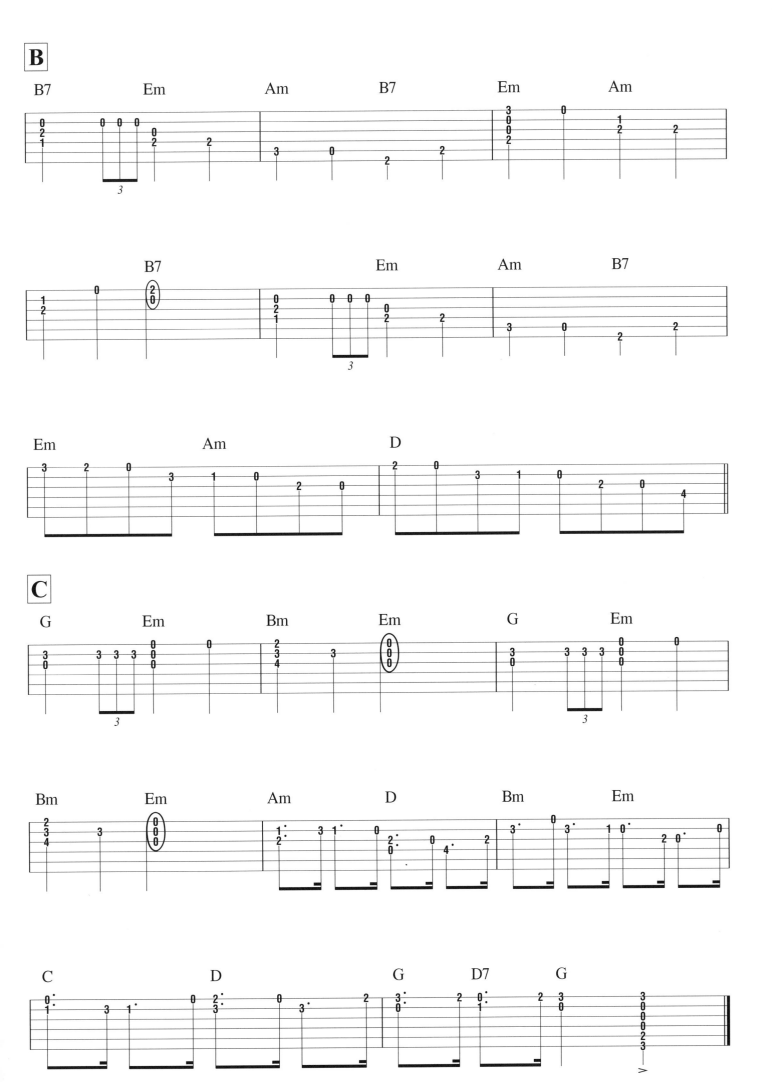

O Christmas Tree

Traditional German Carol

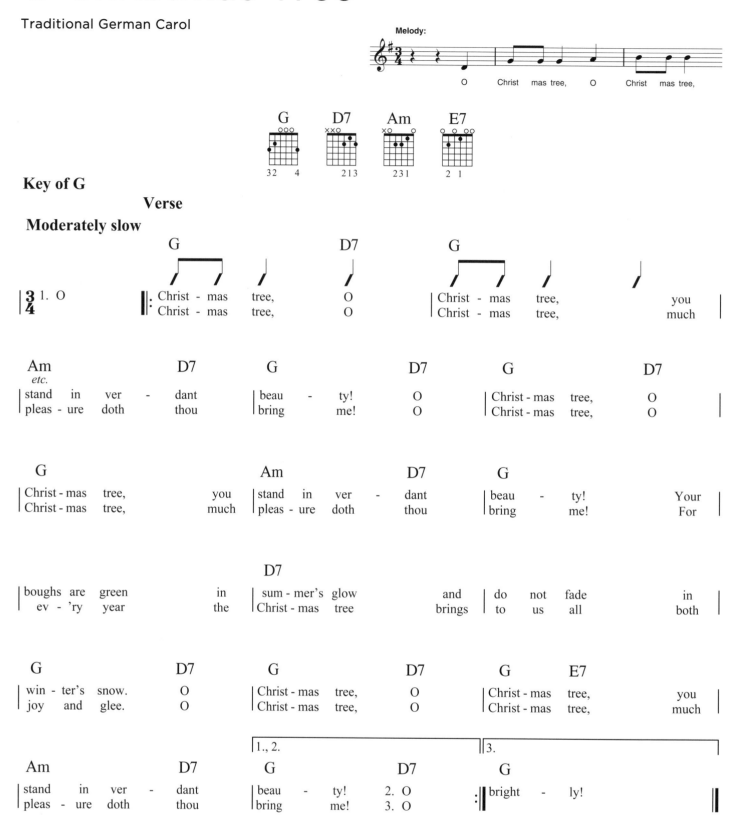

Key of G

Verse

Moderately slow

G		D7	G	
1. O	Christ - mas tree,	O	Christ - mas tree,	you
	Christ - mas tree,	O	Christ - mas tree,	much

Am	D7	G	D7	G	D7
stand in ver - dant	beau - ty!	O	Christ - mas tree,	O	
pleas - ure doth thou	bring me!	O	Christ - mas tree,	O	

G		Am	D7	G	
Christ - mas tree,	you	stand in ver - dant	beau - ty!	Your
Christ - mas tree,	much	pleas - ure doth thou	bring me!	For

		D7			
boughs are green in the	sum - mer's glow and	do not fade in
ev - 'ry year the	Christ - mas tree brings	to us all both

G	D7	G	D7	G	E7
win - ter's snow.	O	Christ - mas tree,	O	Christ - mas tree,	you
joy and glee.	O	Christ - mas tree,	O	Christ - mas tree,	much

1., 2. | | **3.**

Am	D7	G	D7	G
stand in ver - dant	beau - ty!	2. O	bright - ly!
pleas - ure doth thou	bring me!	3. O	

Additional Lyrics

3. O Christmas tree, O Christmas tree,
   Thy candles shine out brightly!
   O Christmas tree, O Christmas tree,
   Thy candles shine out brightly!
   Each bough doth hold its tiny light
   That makes each toy to sparkle bright.
   O Christmas tree, O Christmas tree,
   Thy candles shine out brightly!

O Come, All Ye Faithful
(Adeste Fideles)

Music by John Francis Wade
Latin Words translated by Frederick Oakeley

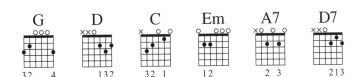

Key of G

Verse
Moderately

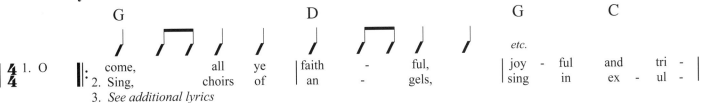

	G			D			G	C
1. O	come,	all ye	faith	- ful,		etc.	joy - ful	and tri -
2. Sing,	choirs of	an	- gels,				sing in	ex - ul -
3. *See additional lyrics*

G		D		Em		A7	D	G
um	- phant.	O		come	ye,	O	come	ye to
ta	- tion.	O		sing	all	ye	cit - i - zens	of

D	A7		D			G	
Beth	-	le -	hem.			Come	and be -
heav'n		a -	bove.			Glo -	ry to

D7	G	D		Em	D		
hold	Him,	born	the	King of	an -	gels. }	O
God		in	the	high -	est. }

Chorus

G				D		G	
come,	let	us	a -	dore	Him. O	come,	let us a -

D		C		A7	D	C
dore	Him. O	come,	let us	a -	dore	Him,

G	D	**1., 2.** G	**3.** G
Christ,	the	Lord!	Lord!

Additional Lyrics

3. Yea, Lord, we greet Thee, born this happy morning.
   Jesus, to Thee be all glory giv'n.
   Word of the Father, now in flesh appearing:

O Come, O Come Immanuel

Plainsong, 13th Century
Words translated by John M. Neale and Henry S. Coffin

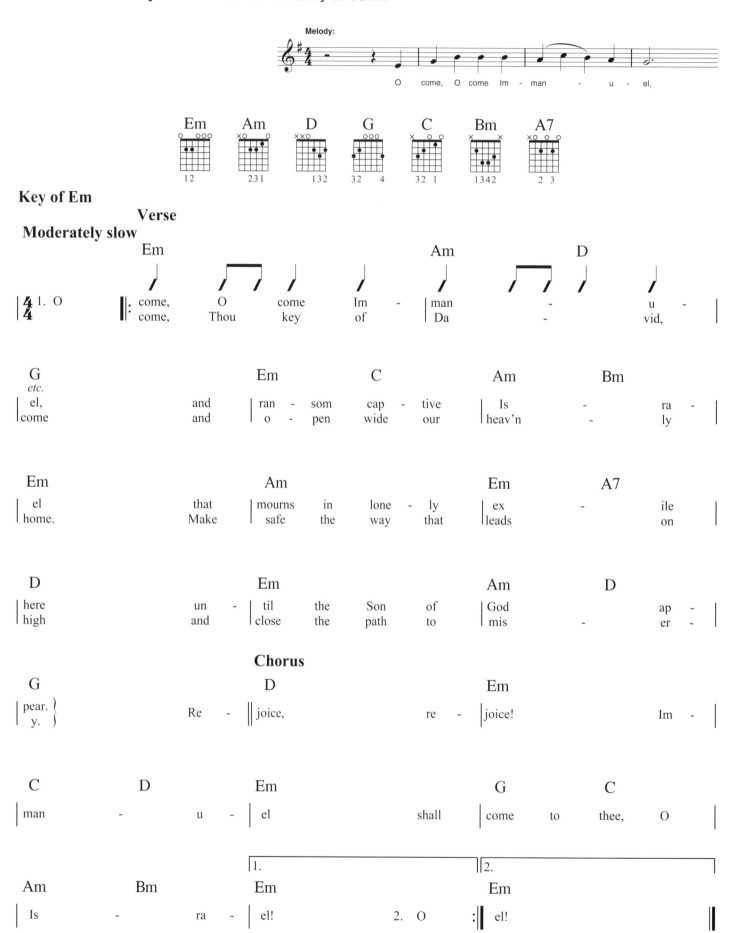

O Little Town of Bethlehem

Words by Phillips Brooks
Music by Lewis H. Redner

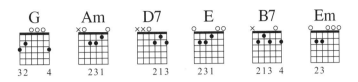

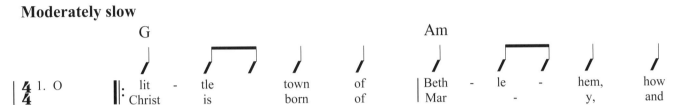

Key of G

Verse
Moderately slow

G
1. O | lit - tle town of | Beth - le - hem, how
Christ is born of | Mar - y, and
3. *See additional lyrics*

G   D7   G   E
etc.
still we see thee | lie!   A - | bove thy deep and
gath - ered all a - | bove,   while | mor - tals sleep, the

Am   G   D7   G
dream - less sleep, the | si - lent stars go | by.   Yet
an - gels keep their | watch of wond - 'ring | love.   O

                              B7   Em
in thy dark streets | shin - eth the | ev - er - last - ing
morn - ing stars, to - | geth - er pro - | claim the ho - ly

B7   G   Am
light.   The | hopes and fears of | all the years are
birth   and | prais - es sing to | God the King and

                                        | 1., 2. | 3.
G   D7   G   G
met in thee to - | night.   2. For   :| el!
peace to men on | earth!   3. O

Additional Lyrics

3. O holy Child of Bethlehem, descend to us, we pray.
Cast out our sin and enter in;
Be born in us today.
We hear the Christmas angels the great glad tidings tell.
O come to us, abide with us
Our Lord, Immanuel!

O Holy Night

French Words by Placide Cappeau
English Words by John S. Dwight
Music by Adolphe Adam

Melody:

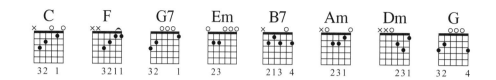

O ho - ly night,

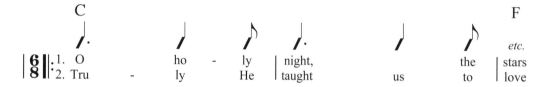

C F G7 Em B7 Am Dm G

Key of C

Verse

Slow, in 2

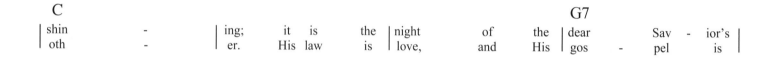

C   F

|6/8 ‖ 1. O   ho - ly   night,   the | stars   are bright - ly |
| 2. Tru - ly   He   taught   us   to | love   one   an - |

C

| shin   - ing;   it   is   the | night   of   the | dear   Sav - ior's |
| oth   - er.   His law is | love,   and His | gos - pel   is |
                                                              G7

C

| birth. | Long   lay   the | world   in |
| peace. | Chains shall He | break,   for   the |

F   C

| sin   and   er - ror | pin   - | ing,   'til   He   ap - |
| slave is   our | broth   - | er,   and   in   His |

Em   B7   Em

| peared   and   the | soul   felt   its | worth. | A |
| name   all   op - | pres - sion shall | cease. | Sweet |

G7   C

| thrill   of | hope,   the | wear - y world   re - | joic - es,   for |
| hymns   of | joy   in | grate - ful cho - rus | raise   we.   Let |

G7					C					
yon	-	der		breaks	a		new	and glor - ious		morn.
all		with -		in	us		praise	His ho - ly		name.

‖

Chorus

Am						Em				
Fall				on	your	knees,			oh,	
Christ				is	the	Lord,			oh,	

Dm						Am				
hear				the an - gel		voic	-	es!		O
praise				His name	for -	ev	-	er!		His

C		G7				C		F		
night				di -		vine,			O	
pow'r				and		glo	-		ry	

C		G7				C				
night				when Christ	was	born.			O	
ev	-			er - more	pro -	claim!			His	

G						C		F		
night,				O		ho	-		ly	
pow'r				and		glo	-		ry	

C		G7				C				
							1.		2.	
night,			O	night	di -	vine!		:‖		‖
ev	-		er -	more	pro -	claim!				

43

Once in Royal David's City

Words by Cecil F. Alexander
Music by Henry J. Gauntlett

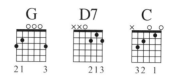

Key of G

Verse

Moderately slow

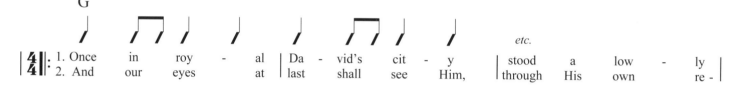

G									
1. Once	in	roy -	al	Da -	vid's	cit -	y	stood	a	low -	ly
2. And	our	eyes	at	last	shall	see	Him,	through	His	own	re -

D7		G							
cat -	tle	shed		where	a	moth -	er	laid	her	ba -	by
deem -	ing	love.		For	that	child	so	dear	and	gen -	tle

			D7		G		C		G
in	a	man -	ger	for	His	bed.	Mar -	y	was	that
is	our	Lord	in	heav'n	a - bove.	And	He	leads	His

D7	G	C		G		1. D7	G		2. D7	G
moth - er	mild,	Je -	sus	Christ	her	lit - tle	child.	He	is	gone.
chil - dren	on	to	the	place	where					

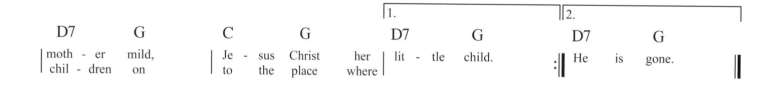

Silent Night

Words by Joseph Mohr
Translated by John F. Young
Music by Franz X. Gruber

Key of G

Verse

Moderately slow

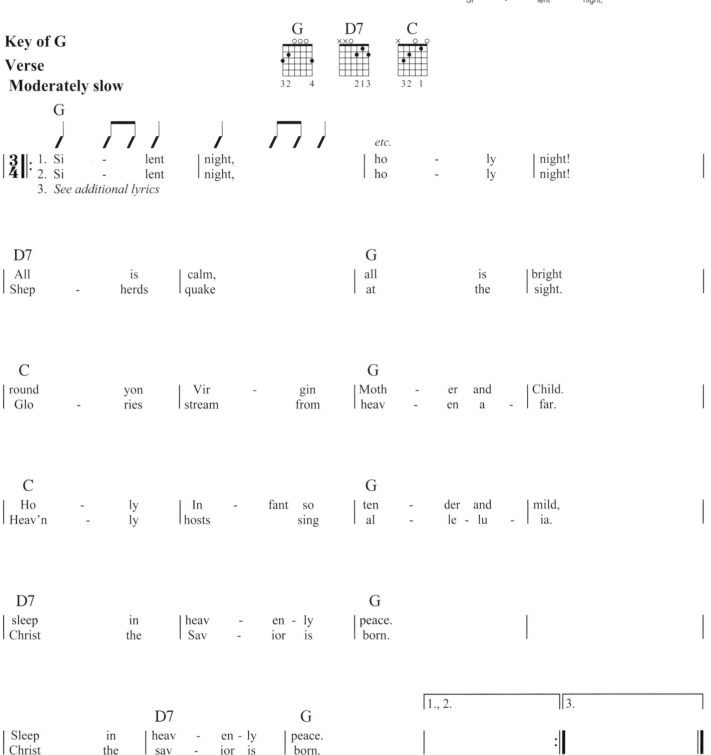

Additional Lyrics

3. Silent night, holy night!
   Son of God, love's pure light.
   Radiant beams from Thy holy face
   With the dawn of redeeming grace.
   Jesus, Lord at Thy birth.
   Jesus, Lord at Thy birth.

Simple Gifts

Traditional Shaker Hymn

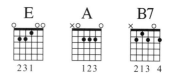

Key of E

Verse
Moderately

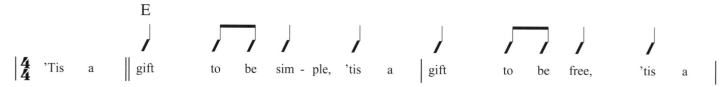

	E									
4/4 'Tis a	gift	to be sim - ple, 'tis a	gift	to be free,	'tis a					

A
etc.

gift	to	come	down	where you ought to	be.	And	when we find our - selves	in the
				B7			E	

place	just	right,	'twill	be	in the val - ley of	love	and de - light.	
				A			E	

When	true	sim -	plic - i - ty	is gained,	to	bow	and to bend	we

won't	be a- shamed.	To	turn,	turn	will	be	our de - light	till by
B7			E					

turn -	ing	and turn -	ing we	come	out	right.	
A		B7		E			

Still, Still, Still

Salzburg Melody, c.1819
Traditional Austrian Text

Still, _____ still, _____ still,

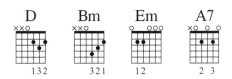

D   Bm   Em   A7

Key of D

Verse

Moderately slow

D		Bm		Em	A7
1. Still,	still,	still,	to	sleep is now His	
2. Sleep,	sleep,	sleep,	while	we Thy vig - il	

D		A7		D	
will.	On	Mar - y's breast He	rests in slum - ber	
keep.	And	an - gels come from	heav - en sing - ing	

A7		D			
while we pray in	end - less num - ber.	Still,	still,	
songs of ju - bi -	la - tion bring - ing	sleep,	sleep,	

Bm		Em	A7	D	1.	2. D
still,	to	sleep is now His	will.		keep.
sleep,	while	we Thy vig - il			

Star of the East

Words by George Cooper
Music by Amanda Kennedy

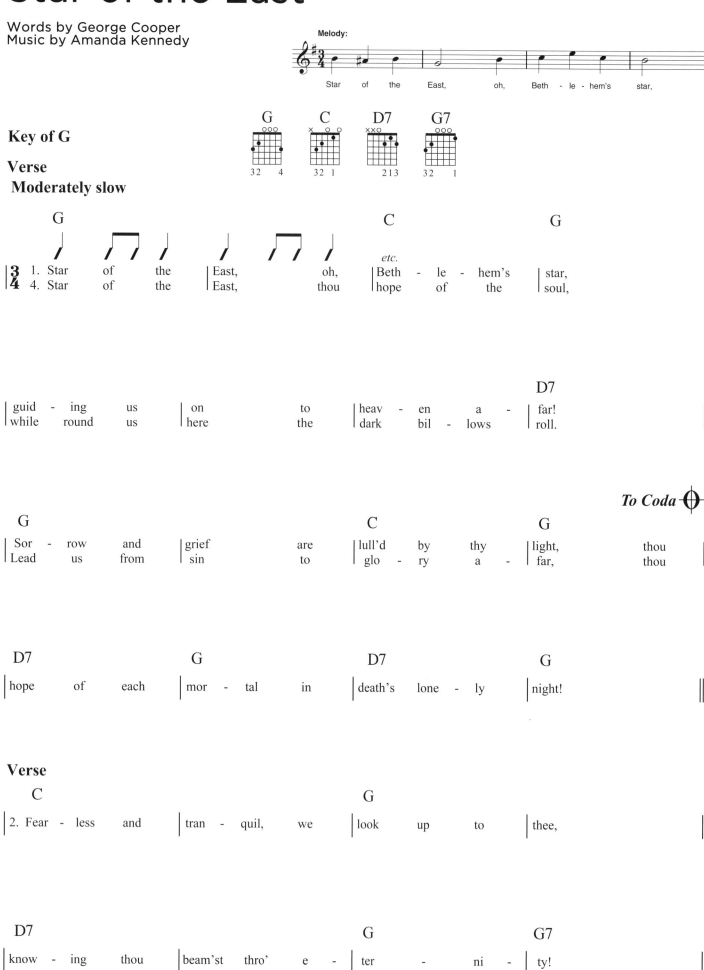

Key of G

Verse
Moderately slow

G				C	G	
1. Star of the	East, oh,	Beth - le - hem's	star,			
4. Star of the	East, thou	hope of the	soul,			

			D7	
guid - ing us	on to	heav - en a -	far!	
while round us here	the	dark bil - lows	roll.	

To Coda

G		C	G		
Sor - row and	grief are	lull'd by thy	light,	thou
Lead us from	sin to	glo - ry a -	far,	thou

D7	G	D7	G	
hope of each	mor - tal in	death's lone - ly	night!	

Verse

C		G		
2. Fear - less and	tran - quil, we	look up to	thee,	

D7		G	G7	
know - ing thou	beam'st thro' e -	ter - ni -	ty!	

C			fol - low where	thou still dost	guide.		
Help	us	to					

G

D7					G		
Pil - grims	of	earth	so	wide.			3. Oh ‖

Verse

G		D7		G		C	G	
star	that	leads	to	God	a - bove,		whose	

D7		G		D7				
rays	are	peace	and	joy	and	love,	watch	

G		D7		G		C	G	
o'er	us	still	'til	life	hath	ceased.	Beam	

D.C. al Coda

D7		G		D7		G		
on,	bright	star,	sweet	Beth - le - hem	star!			‖

Coda

D7		G		D7		G		
star	of	the	East,	thou sweet	Beth - l'em's	star.		‖

49

Sussex Carol

Traditional English Carol

Key of G

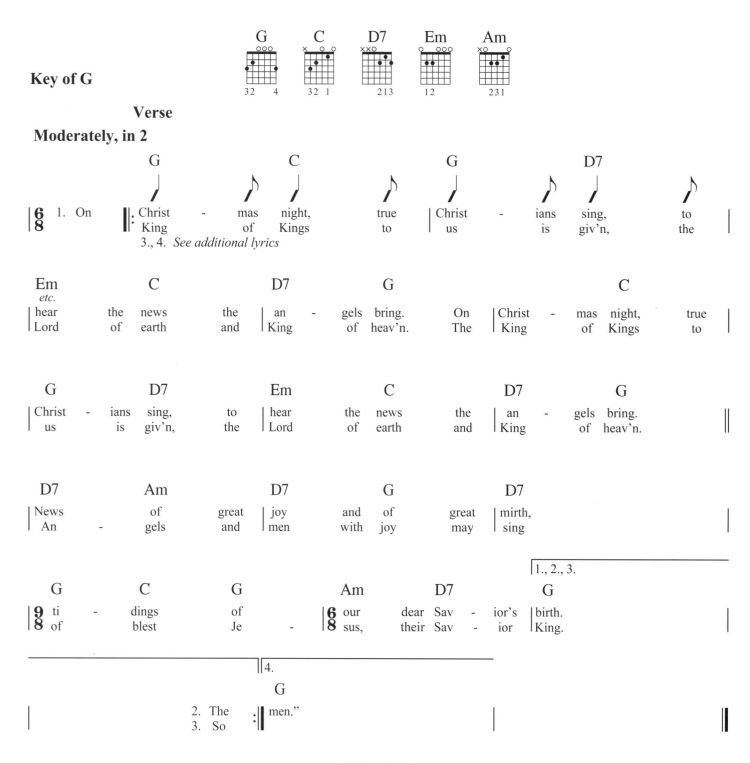

Additional Lyrics

3. So how on earth can men be sad,
   When Jesus comes to make us glad?
   So how on earth can men be sad,
   When Jesus comes to make us glad?
   From all our sins to set us free,
   Buying for us our liberty.

4. From out the darkness have we light,
   Which makes the angels sing this night.
   From out the darkness have we light,
   Which makes the angels sing this night.
   "Glory to God, His peace to men,
   And good will, evermore. Amen."

Up on the Housetop

Words and Music by B.R. Hanby

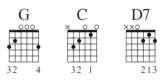

Key of G

Verse
Moderately

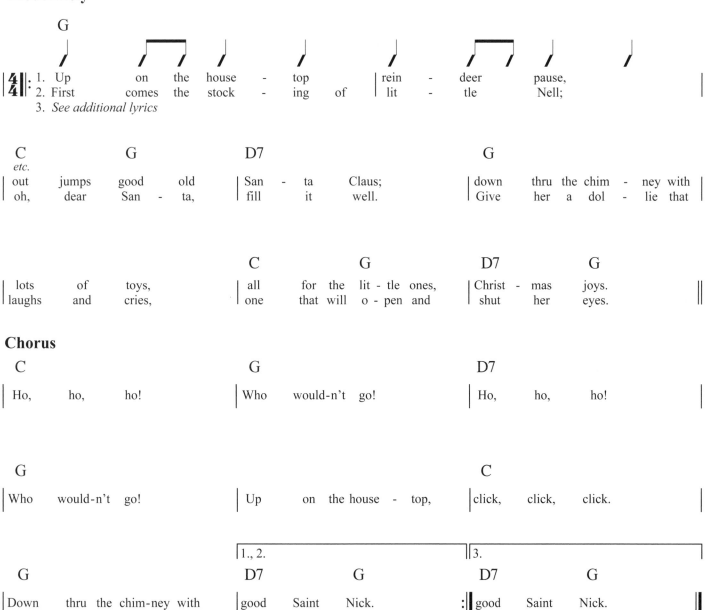

Chorus

C			G			D7		
Ho,	ho,	ho!	Who	would-n't	go!	Ho,	ho,	ho!

G			G			C		
Who	would-n't	go!	Up	on the house - top,		click,	click,	click.

			1., 2.			**3.**		
G			D7	G		D7	G	
Down	thru the chim-ney with		good	Saint	Nick.	good	Saint	Nick.

Additional Lyrics

3. Next comes the stocking of little Will;
   Oh, just see what a glorious fill.
   Here is a hammer and lots of tacks,
   Also a ball and a whip that cracks.

The Twelve Days of Christmas

Traditional English Carol

Melody:

On the   first   day of Christ - mas,   my   true love sent to me:

G   D7   A7   Am

Key of G

Verse
Moderately

G   D7   G

1. On the ‖ first   day   of   Christ - mas,   my ‖ true   love   sent   to   me: a ‖

etc.   D7   G   𝄋 **Verse**   G

‖ par - tridge   in   a   pear ‖ tree.   2. On the ‖ sec - ond day of Christ - mas, my
                                        3., 4. *See additional lyrics*

D7   G   D7   ***Repeat as needed***

‖ true   love   sent   to   me: ‖ 3/4 ‖: two   tur - tle   doves   :‖ 1/4 and a 4/4

|1., 2.   ‖3.
G   D7   G   ***D.S.*** G

4/4 par - tridge   in   a   pear ‖ tree.   3. On the ‖ tree.   5. On the ‖

Verse

G   D7   G   A7

‖ fifth   day of Christ - mas, my ‖ true love sent to me: ‖ five   gold   ‖

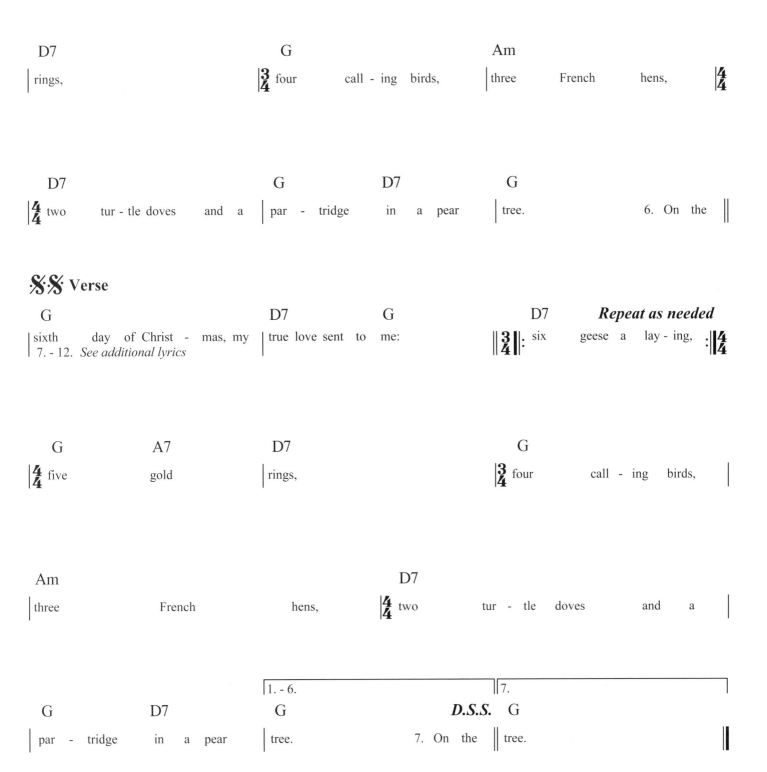

Additional Lyrics

3. On the third day of Christmas, my true love sent to me:
   Three French hens, two turtle doves and a partridge in a pear tree.

4. On the fourth day of Christmas, my true love sent to me:
   Four calling birds, three French hens, two turtle doves and a partridge in a pear tree.

7. On the seventh day of Christmas, my true love sent to me: seven swans a swimming,...

8. On the eighth day of Christmas, my true love sent to me: eight maids a milking,...

9. On the ninth day of Christmas, my true love sent to me: nine ladies dancing,...

10. On the tenth day of Christmas, my true love sent to me: ten lords a leaping,...

11. On the 'leventh day of Christmas, my true love sent to me: 'leven pipers piping,...

12. On the twelfth day of Christmas, my true love sent to me: twelve drummers drumming,...

Ukrainian Bell Carol

Traditional

Key of Am

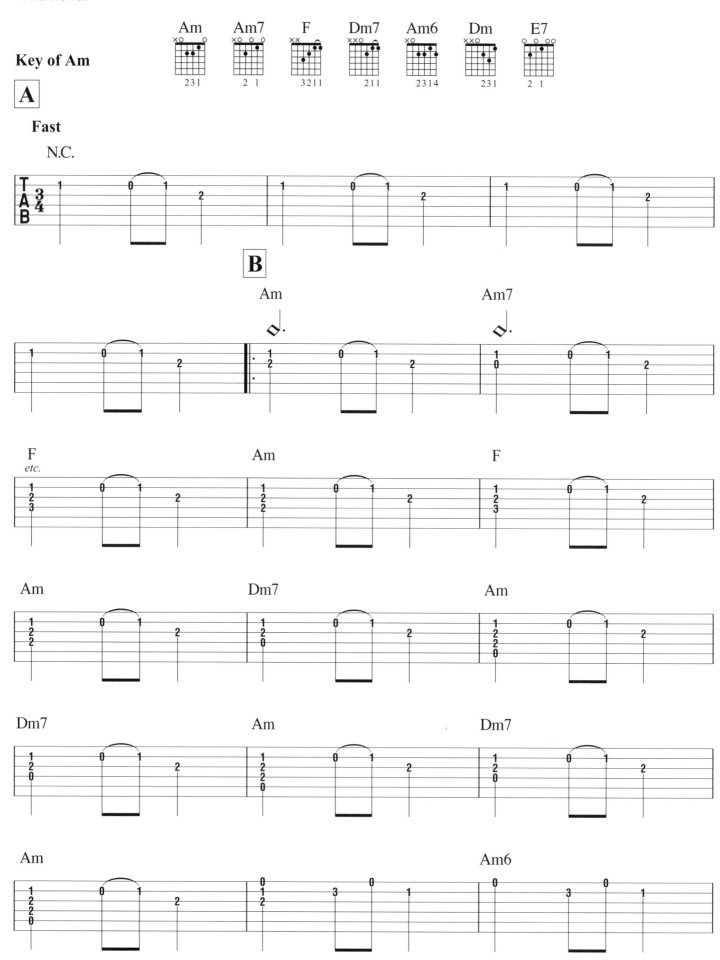

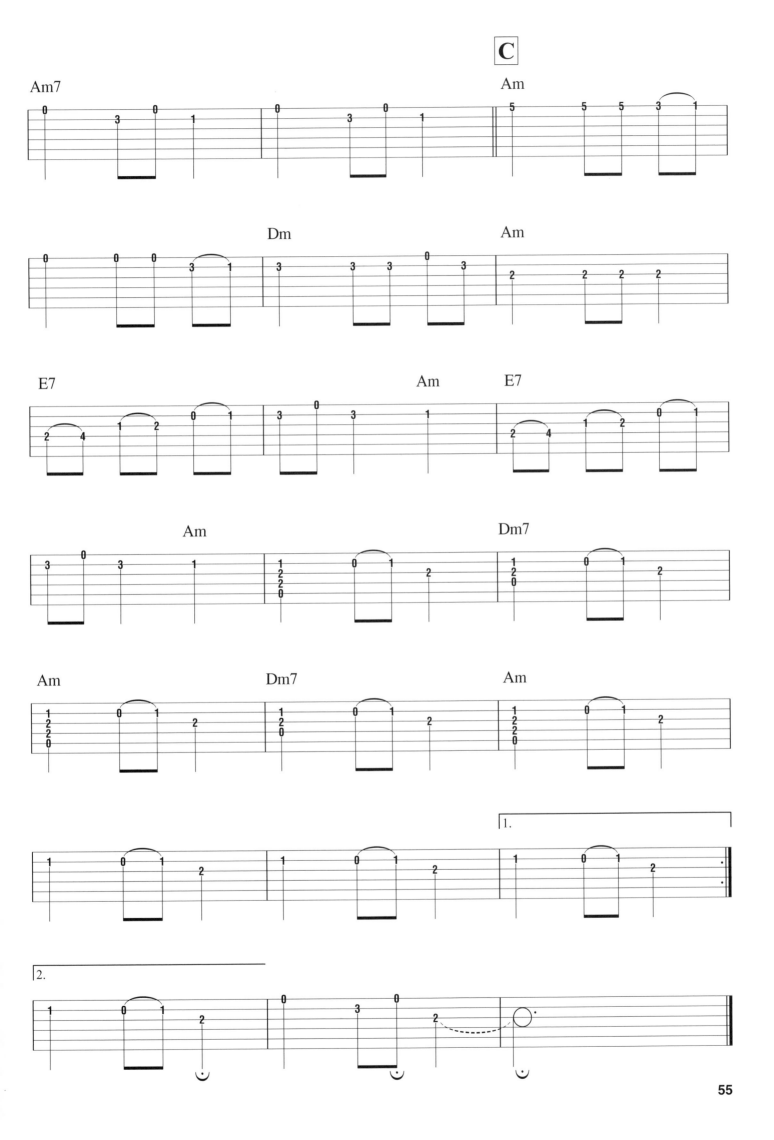

We Three Kings of Orient Are

Words and Music by John H. Hopkins, Jr.

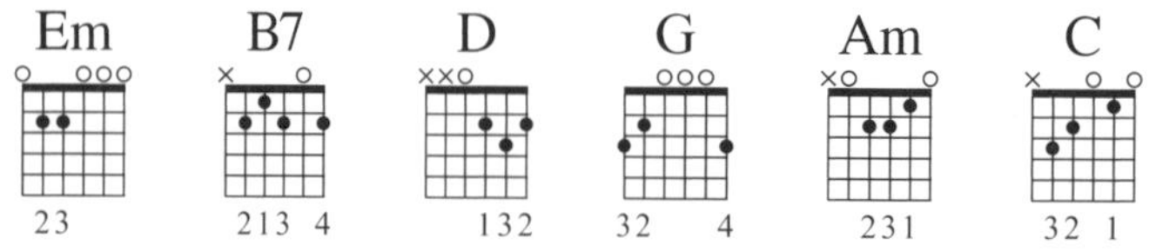

Melody:

We three Kings of Or - i - ent are

Em   B7   D   G   Am   C

Key of Em

Verse
Moderately fast

Em
1. We three Kings of Or - i - ent
2. Born a King on Beth - le - hem
3., 4., 5. *See additional lyrics*

B7
etc.

Em
are bear - ing gifts we
plain, gold I bring to

B7   Em
tra - verse a - far. Field and
crown Him a - gain. King for -

D   G
foun - tain, moor and moun - tain,
ev - er, ceas - ing nev - er,

Am   B7   Em
fol - low - ing yon - der star.
o - ver us all to reign.

Chorus

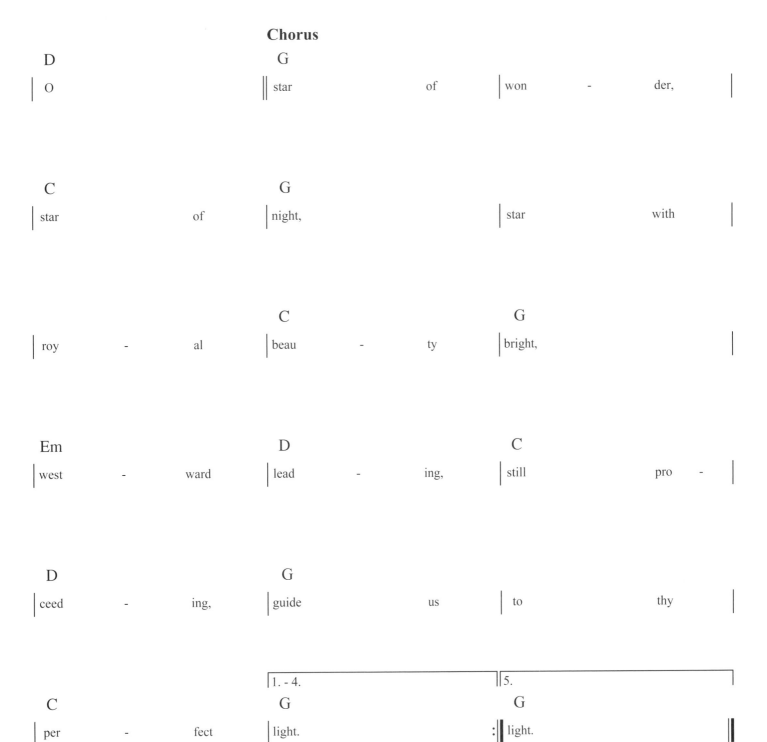

D
| O ‖ star of | won - der,

G

C
| star of | night, star with

G

| roy - al | beau - ty | bright,

C   G

Em
| west - ward | lead - ing, | still pro -

D   C

D
| ceed - ing, | guide us | to thy

G

| 1. - 4. | 5.

C
| per - fect | light.   :‖ light.

G   G

Additional Lyrics

3. Frankincense to offer have I;
   Incense owns a Deity nigh;
   Prayer and praising, all men raising,
   Worship Him, God most high.

4. Myrrh us mine; it's bitter perfume
   Breathes a life of gathering gloom;
   Sorrowing, sighing, bleeding, dying;
   Sealed in the stone-cold tomb.

5. Glorious now, behold Him arise,
   King and God, and Sacrifice!
   Heav'n sings alleluia,
   Alleluia the earth replies:

We Wish You a Merry Christmas

Traditional English Folksong

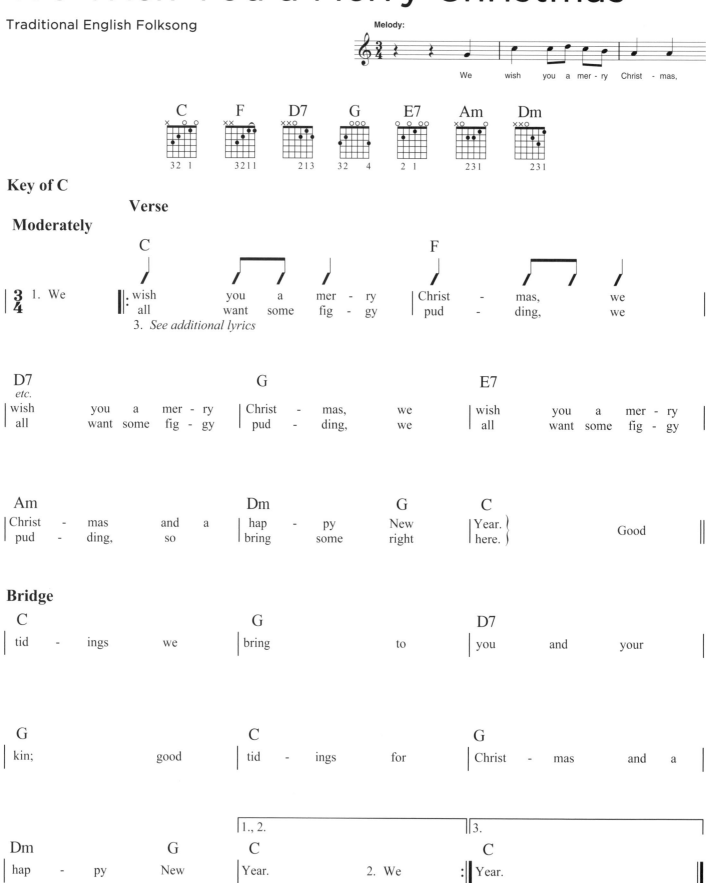

Key of C

Verse

Moderately

3/4 1. We ‖: wish you a mer - ry | Christ - mas, we
      all want some fig - gy | pud - ding, we
      3. *See additional lyrics*

C ... **F**

wish you a mer - ry | Christ - mas, we | wish you a mer - ry
all want some fig - gy | pud - ding, we | all want some fig - gy

D7 *etc.* ... **G** ... **E7**

Christ - mas and a | hap - py New | Year. } Good
pud - ding, so | bring some right | here. }

Am ... **Dm** ... **G** ... **C**

Bridge

C ... **G** ... **D7**

| tid - ings we | bring to | you and your

G ... **C** ... **G**

| kin; good | tid - ings for | Christ - mas and a

Dm ... **G** ... **C** (1., 2.) ... **C** (3.)

| hap - py New | Year. 2. We :‖ Year.

Additional Lyrics

3. We won't go until we get some,
   We won't go until we get some,
   We won't go until we get some,
   So bring some right here.

What Child Is This?

Words by William C. Dix
16th Century English Melody

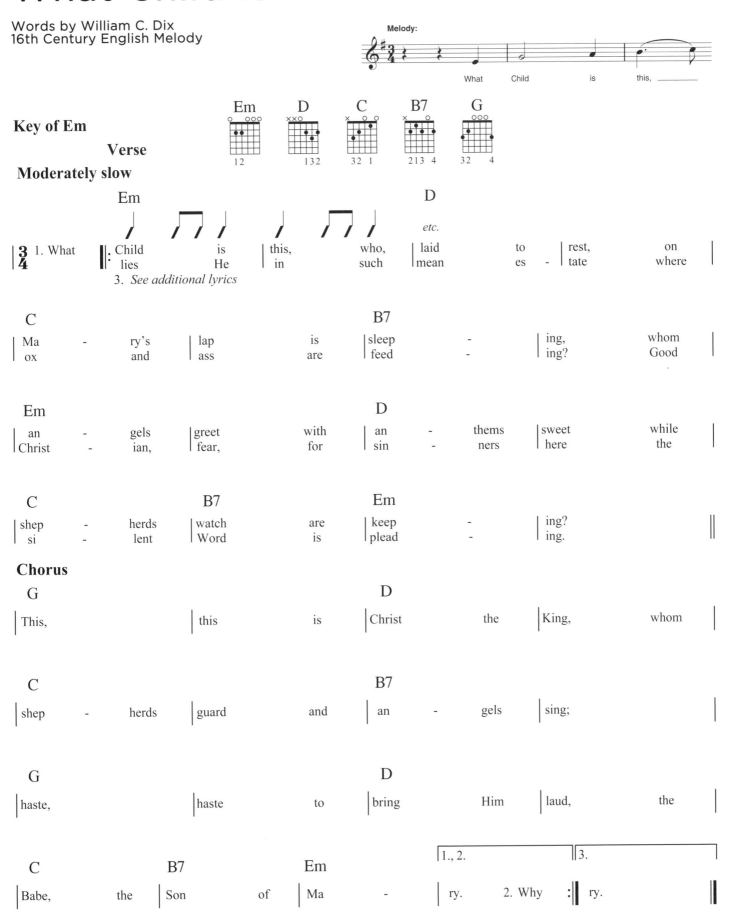

Key of Em

Verse

Moderately slow

Em
1. What | Child is this, who, laid to | rest, on
   lies He in such mean es - | tate, where
3. *See additional lyrics*

C **B7**
Ma - ry's | lap is | sleep - | ing, whom
ox and | ass are | feed - | ing? Good

Em .... **D**
an - gels | greet with | an - thems | sweet while
Christ - ian, | fear, for | sin - ners | here the

C .... **B7** .... **Em**
shep - herds | watch are | keep - | ing?
si - lent | Word is | plead - | ing.

Chorus

G .... **D**
This, | this is | Christ the | King, whom

C **B7**
shep - herds | guard and | an - gels | sing;

G .... **D**
haste, | haste to | bring Him | laud, the

C .... **B7** .... **Em** .... [1., 2.] .... [3.]
Babe, the | Son of | Ma - | ry. 2. Why | ry.

Additional Lyrics

3. So bring Him incense, gold, and myrrh; come peasant King, to own Him.
   The King of kings salvation brings; let loving hearts enthrone Him.

While Shepherds Watched Their Flocks

Words by Nahum Tate
Music by George Frideric Handel

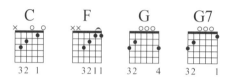

Key of C

Verse

Moderately

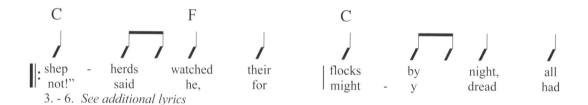

1. While shep - herds watched their flocks by night, all
"not!" said he, for might - y dread all had

3. - 6. *See additional lyrics*

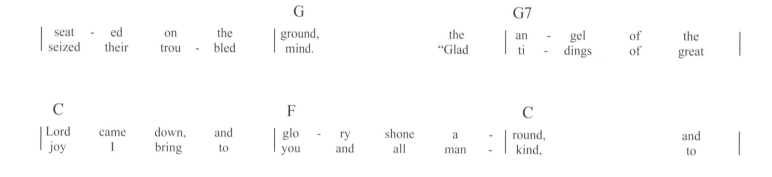

seat - ed on the ground, the an - gel of the
seized their trou - bled mind. "Glad ti - dings of the great

C   F   C
Lord came down, and glo - ry shone a - round, and
joy I bring to you and all man - kind, to

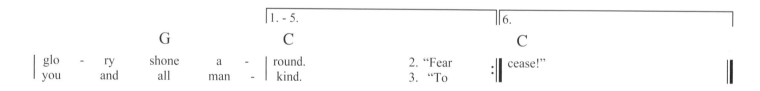

| 1. - 5. | 6. |
G   C   C
glo - ry shone a - round. 2. "Fear cease!"
you and all man - kind. 3. "To

Additional Lyrics

3. "To you, in David's town this day,
Is born of David's line,
The Savior, who is Christ the Lord;
And this shall be the sign,
And this shall be the sign:

4. "The heavenly Babe you there shall find
To human view displayed,
All meanly wrapped in swathing bands,
And in a manger laid,
And in a manger laid."

5. "All glory be to God on high,
And to the earth be peace;
Good will henceforth from heaven to men,
Begin and never cease,
Begin and never cease!"

6. "All glory be to God on high,
And to the earth be peace;
Good will henceforth from heaven to men,
Begin and never cease,
Begin and never cease!"

Celebrate Christmas

WITH YOUR GUITAR AND HAL LEONARD

THE BEST CHRISTMAS GUITAR FAKE BOOK EVER – 2ND EDITION

 INCLUDES TAB

Over 150 Christmas classics for guitar. Songs include: Blue Christmas • The Chipmunk Song • Frosty the Snow Man • Happy Holiday • A Holly Jolly Christmas • I Saw Mommy Kissing Santa Claus • I Wonder As I Wander • Jingle-Bell Rock • Rudolph, the Red-Nosed Reindeer • Santa Bring My Baby Back (To Me) • Suzy Snowflake • Tennessee Christmas • and more.

00240053 Melody/Lyrics/Chords............. $22.50

THE BIG CHRISTMAS COLLECTION FOR EASY GUITAR

Includes over 70 Christmas favorites, such as: Ave Maria • Blue Christmas • Deck the Hall • Feliz Navidad • Frosty the Snow Man • Happy Holiday • A Holly Jolly Christmas • Joy to the World • O Holy Night • Silver and Gold • Suzy Snowflake • and more. Does not include TAB.

00698978 Easy Guitar.............................. $16.95

CHRISTMAS

INCLUDES TAB

Guitar Play-Along Volume 22
Book/Online Audio

8 songs: The Christmas Song (Chestnuts Roasting on an Open Fire) • Frosty the Snow Man • Happy Xmas (War Is Over) • Here Comes Santa Claus (Right Down Santa Claus Lane) • Jingle-Bell Rock • Merry Christmas, Darling • Rudolph the Red-Nosed Reindeer • Silver Bells.

00699600 Guitar Tab................................ $15.99

CHRISTMAS CAROLS

Guitar Chord Songbook

80 favorite carols for guitarists who just need the lyrics and chords: Angels We Have Heard on High • Away in a Manger • Deck the Hall • Good King Wenceslas • The Holly and the Ivy • Irish Carol • Jingle Bells • Joy to the World • O Holy Night • Rocking • Silent Night • Up on the Housetop • Welsh Carol • What Child Is This? • and more.

00699536 Lyrics/Chord Symbols/
            Guitar Chord Diagrams............ $12.99

CHRISTMAS CAROLS

 INCLUDES TAB

Guitar Play-Along Volume 62
Book/CD Pack

8 songs: God Rest Ye Merry, Gentlemen • Hark! The Herald Angels Sing • It Came upon the Midnight Clear • O Come, All Ye Faithful (Adeste Fideles) • O Holy Night • Silent Night • We Three Kings of Orient Are • What Child Is This?

00699798 Guitar Tab................................ $12.95

CHRISTMAS CAROLS

INCLUDES TAB

Jazz Guitar Chord Melody Solos

Chord melody arrangements in notes & tab of 26 songs of the season. Includes: Auld Lang Syne • Deck the Hall • Good King Wenceslas • Here We Come A-Wassailing • Joy to the World • O Little Town of Bethlehem • Toyland • We Three Kings of Orient Are • and more.

00701697 Solo Guitar.............................. $12.99

THE CHRISTMAS GUITAR COLLECTION

INCLUDES TAB

Book/CD Pack

20 beautiful fingerstyle arrangements of contemporary Christmas favorites, including: Blue Christmas • Feliz Navidad • Happy Xmas (War Is Over) • I Saw Mommy Kissing Santa Claus • I'll Be Home for Christmas • A Marshmallow World • The Most Wonderful Time of the Year • What Are You Doing New Year's Eve? • and more. CD includes full demos of each piece.

00700181 Fingerstyle Guitar..................... $17.95

CLASSICAL GUITAR CHRISTMAS COLLECTION

INCLUDES TAB

Includes classical guitar arrangements in standard notation and tablature for more than two dozen beloved carols: Angels We Have Heard on High • Auld Lang Syne • Ave Maria • Away in a Manger • Canon in D • The First Noel • I Saw Three Ships • Joy to the World • O Christmas Tree • O Holy Night • Silent Night • What Child Is This? • and more.

00699493 Guitar Solo.............................. $10.99

FINGERPICKING CHRISTMAS

INCLUDES TAB

Features 20 classic carols for the intermediate-level guitarist. Includes: Away in a Manger • Deck the Hall • The First Noel • It Came upon the Midnight Clear • Jingle Bells • O Come, All Ye Faithful • Silent Night • We Wish You a Merry Christmas • What Child Is This? • and more.

00699599 Solo Guitar................................ $9.99

FINGERPICKING CHRISTMAS CLASSICS

INCLUDES TAB

15 favorite holiday tunes, with each solo combining melody and harmony in one superb fingerpicking arrangement. Includes: Christmas Time Is Here • Feliz Navidad • I Saw Mommy Kissing Santa Claus • Mistletoe and Holly • My Favorite Things • Santa Baby • Somewhere in My Memory • and more.

00701695 Solo Guitar................................ $7.99

FINGERPICKING YULETIDE

INCLUDES TAB

Carefully written for intermediate-level guitarists, this collection includes an introduction to fingerstyle guitar and 16 holiday favorites: Do You Hear What I Hear • Happy Xmas (War Is Over) • A Holly Jolly Christmas • Jingle-Bell Rock • Rudolph the Red-Nosed Reindeer • and more.

00699654 Fingerstyle Guitar..................... $9.99

THE ULTIMATE CHRISTMAS GUITAR SONGBOOK

100 songs in a variety of notation styles, from easy guitar and classical guitar arrangements to note-for-note guitar tab transcriptions. Includes: All Through the Night • Auld Lang Syne • Away in a Manger • Blue Christmas • The Chipmunk Song • The Gift • I've Got My Love to Keep Me Warm • Jingle Bells • One Bright Star • Santa Baby • Silver Bells • Wonderful Christmastime • and more.

00700185 Multi-Arrangements.................. $19.95

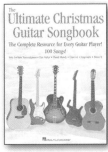

HAL•LEONARD®

www.halleonard.com

Prices, contents and availability subject to change without notice.

0717

HAL•LEONARD® GUITAR PLAY-ALONG

AUDIO ACCESS INCLUDED

INCLUDES TAB

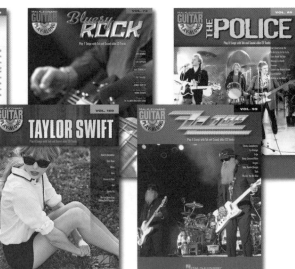

This series will help you play your favorite songs quickly and easily. Just follow the tab and listen to the CD or online audio to hear how the guitar should sound, and then play along using the separate backing tracks. Playback tools are provided for slowing down the tempo without changing pitch and looping challenging parts. The melody and lyrics are included in the book so that you can sing or simply follow along.

HAL•LEONARD®

For complete songlists, visit Hal Leonard online at
www.halleonard.com

Prices, contents, and availability subject to change without notice.

0617

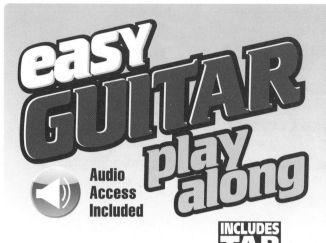

Audio Access Included

INCLUDES TAB

The *Easy Guitar Play Along*® series features streamlined transcriptions of your favorite songs. Just follow the tab, listen to the audio to hear how the guitar should sound, and then play along using the backing tracks. Playback tools are provided for slowing down the tempo without changing pitch and looping challenging parts. The melody and lyrics are included in the book so that you can sing or simply follow along.

1. ROCK CLASSICS

Jailbreak • Living After Midnight • Mississippi Queen • Rocks Off • Runnin' Down a Dream • Smoke on the Water • Strutter • Up Around the Bend.

00702560 Book/CD Pack....... $14.99

2. ACOUSTIC TOP HITS

About a Girl • I'm Yours • The Lazy Song • The Scientist • 21 Guns • Upside Down • What I Got • Wonderwall.

00702569 Book/CD Pack....... $14.99

3. ROCK HITS

All the Small Things • Best of You • Brain Stew (The Godzilla Remix) • Californication • Island in the Sun • Plush • Smells Like Teen Spirit • Use Somebody.

00702570 Book/CD Pack....... $14.99

4. ROCK 'N' ROLL

Blue Suede Shoes • I Get Around • I'm a Believer • Jailhouse Rock • Oh, Pretty Woman • Peggy Sue • Runaway • Wake Up Little Susie.

00702572 Book/CD Pack....... $14.99

6. CHRISTMAS SONGS

Have Yourself a Merry Little Christmas • A Holly Jolly Christmas • The Little Drummer Boy • Run Rudolph Run • Santa Claus Is Comin' to Town • Silver and Gold • Sleigh Ride • Winter Wonderland.

00101879 Book/CD Pack......... $14.99

7. BLUES SONGS FOR BEGINNERS

Come On (Part 1) • Double Trouble • Gangster of Love • I'm Ready • Let Me Love You Baby • Mary Had a Little Lamb • San-Ho-Zay • T-Bone Shuffle.

00103235 Book/CD Pack........ $14.99

8. ACOUSTIC SONGS FOR BEGINNERS

Barely Breathing • Drive • Everlong • Good Riddance (Time of Your Life) • Hallelujah • Hey There Delilah • Lake of Fire • Photograph.

00103240 Book/CD Pack $14.99

9. ROCK SONGS FOR BEGINNERS

Are You Gonna Be My Girl • Buddy Holly • Everybody Hurts • In Bloom • Otherside • The Rock Show • Santa Monica • When I Come Around.

00103255 Book/CD Pack.....$14.99

10. GREEN DAY

Basket Case • Boulevard of Broken Dreams • Good Riddance (Time of Your Life) • Holiday • Longview • 21 Guns • Wake Me up When September Ends • When I Come Around.

00122322 Book/CD Pack $14.99

11. NIRVANA

All Apologies • Come As You Are • Heart Shaped Box • Lake of Fire • Lithium • The Man Who Sold the World • Rape Me • Smells Like Teen Spirit.

00122325 Book/
Online Audio $14.99

12. TAYLOR SWIFT

Fifteen • Love Story • Mean • Picture to Burn • Red • We Are Never Ever Getting Back Together • White Horse • You Belong with Me.

00122326 Book/CD Pack $16.99

13. AC/DC

Back in Black • Dirty Deeds Done Dirt Cheap • For Those About to Rock (We Salute You) • Hells Bells • Highway to Hell • Rock and Roll Ain't Noise Pollution • T.N.T. • You Shook Me All Night Long.

14042895 Book/
Online Audio........$16.99

14. JIMI HENDRIX – SMASH HITS

All Along the Watchtower • Can You See Me • Crosstown Traffic • Fire • Foxey Lady • Hey Joe • Manic Depression • Purple Haze • Red House • Remember • Stone Free • The Wind Cries Mary.

00130591 Book/
Online Audio........$24.99

HAL•LEONARD®
www.halleonard.com

Prices, contents, and availability subject to change without notice.